PENGUIN BOOKS
# THE LAMP IS LIT

Ruskin Bond's first novel, *The Room on the Roof*, written when he was seventeen, received the John Llewellyn Rhys Memorial Prize in 1957. Since then he has written a number of novellas, essays, poems and children's books, many of which have been published by Penguin. He has also written over 500 short stories and articles that have appeared in magazines and anthologies. He received the Sahitya Akademi Award in 1992, the Padma Shri in 1999 and the Padma Bhushan in 2014.

Ruskin Bond was born in Kasauli, Himachal Pradesh, and grew up in Jamnagar, Dehradun, New Delhi and Simla. As a young man, he spent four years in the Channel Islands and London. He returned to India in 1955. He now lives in Landour, Mussoorie, with his adopted family.

# *the lamp is lit*
## *leaves from a journal*

# RUSKIN BOND

**PENGUIN BOOKS**

An imprint of Penguin Random House

PENGUIN BOOKS

USA | Canada | UK | Ireland | Australia
New Zealand | India | South Africa | China | Singapore

Penguin Books is part of the Penguin Random House group of companies
whose addresses can be found at global.penguinrandomhouse.com

Published by Penguin Random House India Pvt. Ltd
4th Floor, Capital Tower 1, MG Road,
Gurugram 122 002, Haryana, India

First published by Penguin Books India 1998

The sketch of a wild pea in flower reproduced on the interleaving pages is by
Ruskin Bond

20 19 18 17 16 15 14 13

The views and opinions expressed in this book are the author's own and the
facts are as reported by him which have been verified to the extent possible,
and the publishers are not in any way liable for the same.

ISBN 9780140278040

Typeset in Palatino by Pooja Printographic, New Delhi

Printed at Repro India Limited

www.penguin.co.in

*Sharing your feelings with friends and companions, you shackle your mind and miss the mark. Watch out for the danger of society, and wander alone like the rhinoceros.*

*When you become involved with a wife and children, you are entangled like a big bamboo tree. Be like a young bamboo tree, and wander alone like the rhinoceros.*

*People keep you company and serve you for motive; real friends are hard to find these days. People are insincere, clever in pursuing their own ends. Wander alone like the rhinoceros.*

— *From* The Rhinoceros Horn Sutra
*Gandhari text, BC 1st century*

\* \* \*

*When I was ten, I was lonely and read books.*
*At fifteen, I played football with other boys.*
*When I was twenty, I courted the girls.*
*At thirty, I thought time had passed too swiftly.*
*When I was forty, I concluded that I was a failure.*
*But at fifty, as I was still alive and well, I knew I*
*    was a success.*
*At sixty, I played old music and fell in love again.*
*At seventy, I went in search of old friends.*

— RB

# Contents

# Contents

# Introduction

There is no escaping the forces of nature.

When Newton sat beneath an apple tree and an apple fell on his head, he discovered the law of gravity. When I sat beneath an apple tree and a large red Himachali apple fell on my head, I discovered that, far from keeping the doctor away, an apple can give you a headache. So I shifted to another tree, a cherry. Cherries don't hurt, unless you eat too many of them. Suffice to say that I like sitting beneath trees : they make me feel younger, and occasionally I can write a poem or a story while enjoying their shade and the gentle flurry of their leaves.

A young reader recently wrote to me, saying: 'I want to be a writer like you, so that I can lie on the grass and do nothing.' Lying on the grass and doing nothing is of course a wonderful occupation, but I did not survive as a freelance writer for over forty years simply by lying on the grass and counting ladybirds. If the grass is to mean anything, a time comes when you have to get up, brush the ladybirds from your shirt and trousers, and proceed to your desk to write, type or word-process all those ideas you get while sitting out there doing nothing.

During my idle moments I receive many good thoughts (and some that are not so good), but these thoughts have to be translated into intelligible and readable language if they are to convey anything to others. And that's where the hard but pleasurable work comes in. The composing, the revising, the rewriting.

The essays and episodes (many taken from my

journals) in this collection may give the reader a picture of my life both as writer and person. In my case they are one and the same thing. I live through my writing, just as my writing lives through me.

This is not autobiography in the fullest sense. In my previous book, *Scenes from a Writer's Life*, I did trace my development as an individual and as a budding writer through my childhood and teens; but there is an equal amount of autobiography to be found in my fiction. The account of my mother's final illness in the story 'The Last Time I Saw Delhi' says more than any factual account that I can give; sometimes it is easier to tell the truth by disguising it as a 'fiction' —especially when the subject is a painful one. . . And perhaps my feelings for my father are best expressed in the short story 'The Funeral', although the funeral is a purely imaginary one; I was at boarding school in Simla when my father died in Calcutta.*

The essays and journal entries presented here are factual and, to some extent, revealing, but they have been put together by me largely as a celebration of my survival as a freelance—this survival being as much the result of my stubbornness and persistence as of any talent that I may possess. I have known many talented young writers who gave up too quickly.

My early forays into literary magazines are described in the first part of this book, along with some examples of my work at the time. Most people think of me as a small-town or hill-station person, for that is what I have become; but I did spend four years

---

* Both stories are to be found in *Delhi Is Not Far: The Best of Ruskin Bond* (Penguin India, 1994)

of my life in London, and five years (summers included) in New Delhi. But it was only when I came to live in the hills, some thirty years ago, that I 'blossomed' into the sort of personal nature writer and children's writer described in my largely autobiographical *Rain in the Mountains*. And I have learnt to laugh at myself. When I was younger, I took myself too seriously.

Recently someone asked me why I did not write on social issues. Well, I had always thought that man's relationship with the natural world *was* a social issue, but apparently he was thinking of issues such as caste, class, religious bigotry, the economic uplift of the masses, etc., all important issues, and all dealt with far more effectively by writers who are more gifted in that direction. I was hoping that there was still room in this world for a simple storyteller, one who strives to give pleasure to both child and adult, not by hiding our scars but by showing that we can be beautiful in spite of them. I find it easier to see God in a raindrop then in a place of worship. My credo, for what it's worth, is given in the last chapter, 'When The Lamp Is Lit.'

Among writers, I am not one of the big guns. I am not even a little gun. I'm just a pebble lying on the beach. But I like to think that I'm a smooth, round, colourful pebble, and that someone will pick me up, derive a little pleasure from holding me, and possibly even put me in his, or her, pocket. Could you be that wanderer by the sea? I shall nestle there, close to you. I shall try to make you feel better. And if you tire of me, you can always throw me back into the sea. Perhaps a kindly wave will wash me ashore again, and someone else will pick me up.

* * *

This extract from my journal may be relevant here:

> It is worth noting that some of the great story writers, like Gorki, were tramps. Stevenson did a lot of tramping before he settled down on his South Sea Island. On one of his tramps through Europe his sole companion was a donkey. They got on famously, and their journey together resulted in a classic travelogue, *Travels With a Donkey*. Wordsworth, wandering lonely as a cloud, tramped about a good deal, all the while recording nature's bounty. Kalidas's wanderings in the Vindhya mountains gave him his incomparable knowledge of nature's ways, described with such loving exactitude in *The Cloud Messenger* and his verse dramas. Whitman's 'Leaves of Grass' celebrates America's great open spaces. Conard tramped the high seas, commanding little tramp steamers, and then held a mirror to the sea in finely crafted novels and romances.
>
> These were lonely men, wanderers rather than travellers. In spirit I have always been one of them, although I wander less today than I did as a young man. Although I have become a stay-at-home, taken up with family concerns and the necessity to make a decent income, I remain at heart a wanderer, and my heroes are Kim, Huck Finn, and Captain Marlowe.
>
> I mention these great literary figures not in order that I might rub shoulders with them (we do that when we read their books)

but simply to show that loneliness is a vital part of the artist's creativity. Even today, surrounded by loved ones, I am often conscious of being alone. Every man is an island, no matter how hard he tries to paddle away. A woman may often have the comfort of a child feeding at her breast; men grow up insecure.

You can be amongst people and still be lonely. The loneliest period of my life consisted of the two years I spent in Jersey, a real island, where I lived with relatives. They were not unkind to me, but we did not really love each other; I suppose I wasn't very loveable in those days! And I yearned for all that I had left behind in India. Alone, I walked the waterfront, the rainswept, windswept sea wall, talking to myself, promising myself that I'd be a published writer some day soon, and return to the sensuous welcoming arms of the land I had left. . . I was only seventeen. But out of my loneliness I produced a novel, raw, naïve and imperfect, but brimming with life and joy and truth, my own truth, for to be true to oneself is to be true to others.

# I

## FREELANCING – THE EARLY YEARS

# Writing for My Life

Money talks—and it's usually saying goodbye.

Most of mine had gone in paying for my passage back to India, and when I arrived in my home town of Dehra Dun I had about eight hundred rupees to show for my three years abroad. It didn't help to find that my stepfather was now bankrupt, and that he and my mother were planning to start a new life in Delhi, free of the encumbrance of a non-functioning motor workshop and unmanageable income tax arrears. If they were hoping that I would return from England with my fortune made, they must have been disappointed. That fifty-pound advance from Andre Deutsch for my first book, *The Room on the Roof*, had melted away, and the book was yet to be published. I'd have to write and sell some short stories and articles, and *soon*, if I was to survive in the India of 1955.

Within a couple of months of my return, my mother and stepfather, school-going brother and half-brothers, handicapped sister, along with my mother's dogs (about six of them) had left for Delhi. I did not accompany them. I had not returned to India in order to live in Delhi. And while I have nothing against dogs, I find it difficult to share a small flat with a number of yapping poms, pekes and dachshunds.

I wanted to be near old friends; I wanted new friends. I wanted the proximity of the hills and rivers. And above all, I wanted the freedom of being my very own person.

Bibiji, my stepfather's first wife, offered me a room and balcony above her small provision store in Astley

Hall. I got on well with Bibiji, a well-built woman from Amritsar who flung sacks of flour around as though they were shuttlecocks. I could see that she had probably been a little too much for my diminutive stepfather. She ran the small store by herself, paying the rent out of her meagre profits. She was understandably bitter about my stepfather's second marriage, and did not have a good word for him or for my mother. Having me stay on the premises and pay her a monthly rent gave her a victory of sorts.

Apart from the room, Bibiji gave me breakfast—mooli or aalu parathas with my favourite shalgam (turnip) pickle. I was never any good as a cook and I took my lunch and dinner in assorted small restaurants and dhabas, ruining my digestion in the process. But these eating places were quite cheap, and for five rupees I could have a decent non-vegetarian meal. And if I stuck to the basics—daal and rice and a vegetable curry—I could eat in three rupees.

Bibiji lived in the back of her shop and seldom came up to my room. As she hadn't been in a position to pay the electricity bill for a couple of years, the connection had been cut and I was without electric light. Not that I particularly cared. I lit candles for a few days; but finding that I could not write or read by candlelight without getting a headache, I bought a kerosene lantern and set it up on my desk.

My 'desk' was really a large dining table on which I spread out my notebooks, paper and typewriter. A couple of smooth rounded stones from the Rispana river bed acted as paperweights. There was a framed photograph of my father—it's still on my desk today, forty years on—and one of Vu-Phuong, the Vietnamese girl to whom I had proposed marriage when I was in

4

London, and from whom I hoped to hear some day. As the months went by and I received no news from her (or of her), the photo moved from its frame into my album and remained there as a memory of a distant dream.

It would have been nice to see Raj again, the Punjabi girl with whom I used to play badminton the year before I left for England. A fine, athletic girl, she used to beat me 15-0, 15-1 (the last point in my favour being an act of mercy on her part), and I used to put up with these walkovers just so that I could be with her. The things we do for love! But now her father, like my stepfather, had lost his money in ill-conceived business ventures and had left Dehra Dun with his family. In the 1950s, Dehra Dun was going through a slump; it would recover only a decade or so later.

Reading and writing by lamplight must have aggravated my already weak eyesight, because I had to start wearing glasses by the time my twenty-first birthday came around. They did nothing to improve my appearance; but passers-by who had previously been but a blur from my balcony lookout, were now more clearly defined, and I wasted a good deal of time gazing at college girls walking or cycling past Astley Hall.

I'd be lying if I said I burnt the midnight oil in my striving to make a living as a freelance writer. If I could manage one thousand words a day, I was satisfied. And this could be accomplished in a couple of hours. Afterwards I'd drop in at the Indiana Café for a cup of coffee. Evenings I'd walk to the clock tower for tikkias or kababs with my friends. The lamp was lit much later, and then I'd jot down stray thoughts and ideas, or write a letter.

Then, as now, I wrote in longhand, and as I wasn't a bad typist, I typed up my own fair copy, making minor revisions as I went along. My more ambitious stories went to *The Illustrated Weekly of India,* then edited by C.R. Mandy, an amiable Irishman who had made the magazine a happy blend of the literary and the artistic, along with some popular entertainment highlighted by a page devoted to pictures of newly-weds; so serious and apprehensive did the young brides and bridegrooms look, that this page was considered even funnier than the jokes column. In 1956, the *Weekly* serialized *The Room on the Roof,* followed a year later by its sequel, *Vagrants in the Valley. The Room* had been written in England, out of my homesickness and longing for India. *Vagrants* was written in Dehra, after my return, and lacked some of the youthful optimism of my first book; but it had more of my sensuality. And Dehra was a sensual sort of place, the summers steamy and sub-tropical. (One of my few regrets in life is that I have never really lived in a steamy, jungle sort of place such as the Malaysian archipelago as described by Conrad in *An Outcast of the Islands* or Tomlinson in *The Sea and the Jungle.* No doubt it's the literary landscape of such regions that appeals to me. Living in these remote outposts may not have been much fun.)

The *Weekly* paid about a hundred rupees for a story. A few of these stories—those that ran to about fifteen minutes of reading time—were also submitted to the BBC in London, where they were broadcast in the Home Service short-story slot. Others went to the *Elizabethan,* an excellent magazine for older children.

I wrote short articles too—on a variety of subjects,

ranging from ghosts to buffaloes—and some of these were published in *The Sunday Statesman*, *The Hindu* and *The Tribune*. I was also quite adept at finding new, offbeat markets for my work. *Sainik Samachar* (the Armed Forces weekly) provided a home for some of my stories. I never met anyone who read *Sainik Samachar*, and I doubt if the Defence Ministry even knew that they were its publishers; but it paid me twenty-five rupees for a thousand words, and that was good enough for me. About five years later, when I was living in Delhi, I located its office in a dingy corner of a government building, and met its editor, an elderly, defeated individual who put the magazine together entirely on his own. Mountains of back issues climbed towards the ceiling. The editor confessed that no one read the paper, but that it gave him a salary and in a year's time he would be eligible for a pension. He died before he could start enjoying the pension, and the magazine seemed to go into limbo.

Then there was *The Leader*, a newspaper published from Allahabad. It did not want fiction or literary pieces, but it was willing to publish articles on the entertainment industry. So I sent them a regular 'Letter from Hollywood'. This was easy I was still subscribing to my favourite film magazine, *Picturegoer*, published from London (and now, alas, no more) and all I had to do was cull some of the information about exciting new stars and their films, and string this together into a fresh and readable piece. It was used fortnightly and brought me thirty rupees. This was Grub Street with a vengeance, but I did not remain a Hollywood correspondent for long. My London publisher, Andre Deutsch, informed me that he had sold the German rights in my first novel, *The Room on the Roof*. It turned out to be a tidy sum, and enabled me to write a short novel and a few spontaneous yet carefully crafted stories. Some of them are still around today.

# All You Need Is Paper

As I write, a bright yellow butterfly flits in through the open window and settles on my writing pad. I pause for a moment, wait for the butterfly to make its way across the page and on to a slim copy of Tagore's *Crescent Moon*, which I was reading again last night. I have entered a period of my life when I enjoy returning to old favourites, old classics. Just as there are exciting new authors being brought to our attention every day, so there are exciting *old* authors who have yet to be discovered. Life is too short to take in all of them. It's the beauty of language that draws me back, time and again, to the heart-stopping prose of Conrad in 'Heart of Darkness' and 'Youth'; the lyrical intensity of Emily Brontë in *Wuthering Heights;* the wonderful abandon of Sterne; the precision of Wilde; the broad humour of Dickens and Wells; the rolling, orchestrated prose of T.E. Lawrence in *The Seven Pillars of Wisdom.*

But to return to the butterfly. It takes me back to the little flat in Dehra Dun, where the adventure of being a writer really got under way.

I had grown used to living on my own in small rooms furnished with other people's spare beds, tables and chairs. I had grown used to the print of Constable's 'Blue Boy' on the wall, even though I had never cared for the look of that boy. But those London bedsitters had been different. Whether in Hampstead, Belsize Park, Swiss Cottage or Tooting, they had been uniformly lonely. One seldom encountered any other lodgers, except when they came to complain that my radio was too loud; and the landlady was seen only when the rent fell due. If you wanted company, you went out into the night. If you wanted a meal, you walked down the street to the nearest restaurant or snack bar. If you wanted to kill time, you sat in a cinema. If you wanted a bath, you went round to the nearest public bathing rooms where, for 2s.6d., you were given a small cake of soap, a clean towel, and a tub of piping hot water. The tub took me back to my childhood days in Jamnagar, where I would be soaped and scrubbed by a fond ayah; but there was no fond ayah in London. And rooms with attached baths were rare—and expensive. . .

In contrast, my room over Rajpur Road was the very opposite of lonely. There was the front balcony, from which I could watch the activity along the main road and the shops immediately below me. I could also look into the heart of a large peepal tree, which provided shelter to various birds, squirrels and other small creatures. There were flats on either side of mine, served by a common stairway—and blocked, at night, by a sleeping cow, over whom one had to climb, for it would move for no one. And there were quarters at the back, occupied by servants' families or low-income tenants.

Where should I begin?

I suppose my most colourful neighbour was Mrs Singh, an attractive woman in her thirties, who smoked a hookah. She came from a village near Mainpuri. Her husband was a sub-inspector in the police. They had one son, Anil, a lollipop-sucking brat without any charm. Mrs Singh often regaled me with tales of the supernatural from her village, and I did not hesitate to work some of them into my own stories.

At twilight, sitting on her string cot and puffing at the hookah, she would launch into an account of the various types of ghosts that one might encounter: *churels*, the ghosts of immoral women, who appeared naked with their feet facing backwards; ghosts with long front teeth who sucked human blood; and ghosts who took the form of snakes and animals. I was keen to meet a *churel*, as I thought she would be rather attractive; but all the girls in Dehra had their feet facing forwards.

One species that I found particularly interesting was the *munjia* (supposedly the disembodied spirit of a brahmin youth who had died before his marriage) who takes up his abode in the branches of a lonely peepal tree. When the *munjia* is annoyed, he rushes out of the tree and upsets tongas, bullock-carts and cycles. Mrs Singh said she'd even been in a bus that had been overturned by a *munjia*. She warned me that anyone passing beneath a peepal tree at night must be careful not to yawn without covering his mouth or snapping his fingers in front of it. If he forgets to take this precaution, the *munjia* dashes down his throat and presumably ruins his digestion.

Summer nights I slept on the balcony, in full view of our own peepal tree; but apparently it was not lonely enough for a *munjia*, and I suffered from no ill effects. Anil, who would sometimes insist on sleeping beside me, slept with his mouth open and frequently swallowed moths, termites and other winged creatures, and as his digestion was immune to this fare, it must also have been immune to the attentions of a *munjia*.

Mrs Singh once told me of the night she had seen the ghost of her husband's first wife. The ghost had lifted Anil, then a few months old, out of his cradle, rocked the baby in her arms for a little while, and announced that she was glad the child was a boy—a sentiment not shared by those who knew the eleven-year-old.

Mrs Singh taught me the following mantra, which I was to recite whenever I felt threatened by ghosts or malignant spirits:

> *Bhut, pret, pisach, dana,*
> *Chhoo mantar, sab nikal jana,*
> *Mano, mano, Shiv ka kahna —*

which, roughly translated, goes:

> Ghosts and spirits assembled here,
> Great Shiv is coming—flee in fear!

If I was working at my desk, and saw Anil approaching, I would recite the mantra under my breath. It may have worked on *bhuts* and *prets*, but it had no effect on Anil.

Where, then, were the noble young friends I had written about in my first, semi-autobiographical novel? Well, Somi's family had moved to Calcutta, and Kishen's to Bombay. Dehra, then, was not a place for young men in search of a career. As soon as they finished school or college, they usually took wing. The town was a sleepy hollow, a great place in which to be educated, but a poor place to earn a living.

But there were others to take their place — teenagers struggling to do their Matric or Intermediate, or young men at college, aspiring for their Arts or Science degrees. College was a bit of a dead end. But those who had their schooling in Dehra, and then moved on, usually did well for themselves.

Take just two from Dilaram Bazaar. Gurbachan was an average student, but after doing his Intermediate he went to stay with an uncle in Hong Kong. Ten years later, he was a superintendent in the Income Tax Department. And then there was Narinder, always having to take tuitions to scrape through his exams. But he spoke English quite well, and he had a flair for business. Today, he owns the largest wholesale wine business in the UK. And as he doesn't drink himself, it's profit all the way.

These boys, and others like them, came from middle-class families. It was impossible, then, to foresee what life held in store for them. And it wasn't always happy endings. Sudheer, a charming young scamp, went on to become the assistant manager of a tea estate in Jalpaiguri, and was killed by the tea-garden labourers. Kishen, as a boy, was not the stuff that heroes are made of; but at forty he died while trying to save a child from drowning.

My own future was a little easier to predict. In a sense, I had already arrived. At twenty I was a published author, although not many people had heard of me! And although I wasn't making much money then, and probably never would, it was the general consensus among my friends that I was an impractical sort of fellow and that I would be wise to stick to the only thing that I could do fairly well— putting pen to paper.

I couldn't drive a car. I fell off bicycles. I couldn't repair an electrical fault. My efforts to buy vegetables in the mandi were the cause of great merriment. And my attempts at making a curry sent everyone into paroxysms of laughter. It's true that I added a tablespoon of sugar to the aalu-gobi that I attempted to cook. I thought it improved the flavour. Gujaratis would have approved. But it had no takers in Dehra apart from myself.

On the plus side, I could type, draft job applications for all and sundry, help lovesick students write passionate letters to girls, make my own bed (something I'd learnt at boarding school), walk great distances, and pay for the chaat and tikkias we consumed near the clock tower. I held the tikkia-eating record, having on one occasion put away no less than thirty of these delicious potato patties. Naturally, acute indigestion followed, and it was months before I could face another tikkia.

\* \* \*

Here I must record my first and last foray into the world of commerce.

On Bibiji's insistence that I could make more money from selling vegetables than from selling stories, I thought—why not do just that, sell vegetables? Bibiji said I could sell the vegetables outside her shop, provided I gave her a ten per cent commission. As this was the same commission that a literary agent took, it seemed fair enough.

It only remained for me to get up at five in the morning and march off to the sabzi mandi, there to spend a hard-earned two hundred rupees in stocking up with cauliflowers, carrots and other cold-weather vegetables.

With some help from Mrs Singh's son, Anil, these were neatly displayed outside Bibiji's shop, and on that first day we even had a couple of customers. But housewives do not like breaking the habits of a lifetime, and they continued shopping for their vegetables in the mandi and elsewhere. By the third day my vegetables were looking very sorry for themselves. Anil kept splashing water over them, but they could not be revived. That evening they were all given away to my friends from the Dilaram Bazaar, and my brief venture into the grocery business was at an end.

Was it, I wonder, a throwback to my grandfather's early days as an apprentice to a London grocer? He found soldiering more to his liking. And as a foot soldier, he tramped all over India. I was another kind of soldier, a freelance with a fountain pen, a champion of Grub Street, a seeker after romance in the most unlikely places. The rewards would be meagre, but the freedoms great.

# Summertime in Old New Delhi

I left Dehra for Delhi in 1959, and lived in the capital for a few years—freelancing, and for a time working with an international relief agency. I could not fall in love with Delhi, my heart was always in the hills and small towns of north India.

But there were things I came to like about Delhi, even in summer. The smell of a hot Indian summer is one smell that can never be forgotten. It is not just the thirsty earth with its distinctive odour, but all other ingredients of a hot weather in the plains that go to make this season almost intolerable on the one hand and sweetly memorable on the other. For who can forget that summer brings the jasmine, whose sweet scent drifts past us on the evening breeze along with the stronger odours and scents of mango blossom, raat-ki-rani and cowdung smoke.

Although I have spent most of my life in the hills, I grew up in some fairly hot places—humid Kathiawar ports, dusty old New Delhi, and the steamy Terai— and I am no stranger to prickly heat, mosquito bites, intermittent fever and dysentery and other hot-weather afflictions. Today's residents of the capital complain of pollution and overcrowding, and I wouldn't exchange my mountain perch for the pleasure of being fried crisp, but at least half of them have air-conditioning, coolers, refrigerators and other means to keep the heat at bay. In 1940s' Delhi you were lucky to have a small table-fan, and that was effective only if the bhisti, or water-carrier, came around with his goat-skin bag, splashing water on to the khas-khas matting draped from your door or window; otherwise the fan simply blew hot air at you. I was in Delhi in the early '40s, living with my father, and I shall never forget the fragrant, refreshing smell of the wet khas-reed which cooled the rooms and verandas of New Delhi bungalows (the only high-rise building was the Qutab Minar).

My father and I lived in a small RAF hutment on the fringe of the scrub jungle near Humayun's tomb. This was then furthest Delhi, where one could expect to find peacocks in the garden and a snake in the bathroom. The bhisti and the khas-khas helped us to survive that summer. As did the box-like wind-up gramophone on which I played endless records which had to be stored flat in order to prevent them from warping and assuming weird shapes in the heat. My father liked opera, and on his day off he would play his Caruso records. It was strange to lie beside him on a perspiration-soaked bed, listening to Caruso sing *Che Gelida Manina*:

> *Your tiny hand is frozen,*
> *Let me warm it into life!*

I was nine, a child of warm climates, and I had no idea what it was like to have one's hand frozen. Dipping my hands in ice-cream was the nearest I'd come to it.

In 1959 I was living on the outskirts of a greater, further New Delhi. The influx of refugees from the Punjab after Partition had led to many new colonies springing up on the outskirts of the capital, and at the time the furthest of these was Rajouri Garden. Needless to say, there were no gardens. The treeless colony was buffeted by hot, dusty winds from Haryana and Rajasthan. The houses were built on one side of the Najafgarh Road. On the other side, as yet uncolonized, were extensive fields of wheat and other crops still belonging to the original inhabitants. In an attempt to escape the city life that constantly oppressed me, I would walk across the main road and into the fields, finding old wells, irrigation channels, camels and buffaloes, and sighting birds and small creatures that no longer dwelt in the city. In an odd way, it was my reaction to city life that led to my taking a greater interest in the natural world. Up to that time, I had taken it all for granted.

The notebook I kept at the time is before me now, and my first entry describes the bluejays or rollers that were so much a feature of those remaining open spaces. At rest, the bird is fairly nondescript, but when it takes flight it reveals the glorious bright blue wings and the tail, banded with a lighter blue. It sits motionless. . . But the large dark eyes are constantly watching the ground in every direction. A grasshopper or cricket has only to make a brief appearance, and the bluejay will launch itself straight at its prey. In the spring and early summer the 'roller' lives up to its other name. It indulges in love flights in which it rises and falls in the air with harsh grating screams— a real rock-'n'-roller!

Some way down the Najafgarh Road was a large village pond and beside it a magnificent banyan tree. We have no place for banyan trees today, they need so much space in which to spread their limbs and live comfortably. Cut away its aerial roots and the great tree topples over—usually to make way for a spacious apartment building. That was the first banyan tree I got to know really well. It had about a hundred pillars supporting the boughs, and above them there was this great leafy crown like a pillared hall. It has been said that whole armies could shelter in the shade of an old banyan. And probably at one time they did. I saw another sort of army visit the banyan by the village pond when it was in fruit. Parakeets, mynas, rosy pastors, crested bulbuls without crests, barbets and many other birds crowded the tree in order to feast noisily on big, scarlet figs. Season's eatings!

Even further down the Najafgarh Road was a large jheel, famous for its fishing. I wonder if any part of the jheel still exists, or if it got filled in and became a part of greater Delhi. One could rest in the shade of a small babul or keekar tree and watch the kingfisher skim over the water, making just a slight splash as it dived and came up with small glistening fish. Our common Indian kingfisher is a beautiful little bird with a brilliant blue back, a white throat and orange underparts. I would spot one perched on an overhanging bush or rock, and wait to see it plunge like an arrow into the water and return to its perch to devour the catch. It came over the water in a flash of gleaming blue, shrilling its loud 'tit-tit-tit'.

The kingfisher is the subject of a number of legends, and the one I remember best, recounted by Romain Rolland, tells us that it was originally a plain grey bird that acquired its resplendent colours by flying straight towards the sun when Noah let it out of the Ark. Its upper plumage took the colour of the sky above, while the lower was scorched a deep russet by the rays of the setting sun.

Summer and winter, I scorned the dust and the traffic, and walked all over Delhi—from Rajouri

Garden to Connaught Place, which must have been five or six miles, and on other occasions, from Daryaganj to Chandni Chowk, and from Ajmeri Gate to India Gate! That is the best way to get to know a city. I had walked all over London. Now I did the same thing in Delhi, investigating old tombs and monuments, historic streets and buildings, or simply sitting on the grass near India Gate and eating jamuns. I liked the sour tang of the jamun fruit which was best eaten with a little salt. And I liked the deep purple colour of the fruit. Jamuns were one of the nicer things about Delhi.

# Walking the Streets of Delhi

I made my home in Mussoorie in 1963, but of course I was to revisit Delhi may times, even spending a couple of winters there.

On one of these visits, in 1971, I reached my friend Kamal's house in Rajouri Garden, and mentioned that I had walked from Connaught Place, a distance of some eight miles. His family greeted me with a pained and bewildered silence.

Finally my friend's mother, a practical Punjabi lady, asked: 'How did you lose your money?' She kept hers knotted in the end of her sari, and firmly believed that people who kept their money in easily snatched handbags and wallets were asking for trouble.

'I haven't lost anything,' I said.

'Aren't the buses running?'

'Oh, the buses are running. One nearly ran over me.'

'Then why did you walk?'

'I thought I'd see more that way.'

The rest of the story is told in my journal:

The consensus of opinion in my friend's house is that I am a little mad. They have never heard of anyone in Delhi walking from choice. They prefer to wait long periods for overcrowded buses and hang on by their eyebrows, even if the distance to be covered is only a furlong. As in big cities the world over, the people of Delhi are rapidly losing the use of their legs.

I suppose Delhi is one of the least attractive cities

in which to walk about. Crossing roads can be hazardous. Single- and double-decker buses (many emitting smokescreens of diesel fumes), wildly driven taxis, unpredictable scooter-rickshaws, slow-moving cars and tongas, and thousands of wavering, wayward cyclists, make for chaos on the streets. On the main roads the traffic is fast and furious, and cyclists are frequently knocked over and killed. But Delhi has an acute transport problem, and the cycle is the poor man's only guarantee of getting to work in time. He cannot afford a scooter, and he cannot wait for a bus. And yet, in this city bursting with the Punjabi *nouveau riche* there are thousands who do have their own scooters and cars, and the number and variety of vehicles on the road increase at an alarming rate.

Setting out on another long walk, I realized that the pavement is meant for almost every purpose except walking. I am on the Najafgarh Road, heading in the general direction of central Delhi. It is a straight road, but this is no straight walk. To find a thirty-yard stretch of unoccupied pavement is most unlikely. In a territory where every square foot of land has a high price, why should so much good pavement go to waste?

The first two wayside stalls belong to sellers of lottery tickets. Theirs is a thriving business. All over Delhi, at almost every street corner, there is someone selling lottery tickets. The prizes are attractive enough. The owner of the winning ticket collects Rs 250,000—sometimes more—and there are a number of other prizes. And the income accruing to the state is also tremendous—so much so that almost every state in the country, including Delhi, has climbed on the lottery bandwagon. After all, it is easier than collecting taxes.

No one, not even the street sweeper, grudges giving a rupee to the government if there is a chance in a million of his winning a fortune.

While the poor man is quite willing to part with his rupee, it is the rich man, the thriving businessman, who often goes in for lottery tickets in a big way, sometimes buying up forty or fifty tickets at a time. He believes that while it is great to be rich, there is nothing like getting richer.

How times have changed. Ten years ago, if I asked a Sikh boy what he would like to be on growing up, he would unhesitatingly have said, 'I'll join the Army'—or the Navy, or the Air Force. He was proud of his martial traditions. Yesterday, while talking to an intelligent twelve-year-old Sikh, I asked the same question, and received this reply: 'I'll open a cinema, or deal in spare parts.'

No spirit of adventure, no vision of faraway places—unless it be of a cloth shop in Bangkok! The boy confessed that what he really wanted in life was a television set bigger and better than his neighbour's.

But Delhi is not entirely Punjabi. Here on the Najafgarh Road I find a community of Lohiawalas, a gypsy tribe of blacksmiths who have wandered into Delhi, camped on the pavement, and gone about their ancient and traditional way of living, supremely indifferent to the fast pace, the noise of traffic, the neon signs and Western clothes that surround them on all sides. Their bullock-carts (in which they travel and sleep and live and die and have their babies) stand just off the pavement; these are lined with old iron stamped with decorative patterns and studded with coloured stones.

A charcoal fire has been made in a hole in the

ground, and this is kept alive by a bellows worked by a wheel turned by an attractive woman wearing a black blouse and black skirt. This sombre attire is set off by heavy silver anklets and a pair of very lively eyes. Another pair of bellows has been fashioned out of goat's skin. A man is beating out a strip of red-hot tin on his anvil. A boy is filling a bent bicycle-pump with sand (to keep it firm) before straightening it out with his hammer. The entire family, including bearded old men, wizened old women ready to take off on broomsticks, and naked grandchildren, is at work. Handsome people these; and although they live in dirt and squalor, they seem quiet and dignified.

A little farther along the road are some people making what appear to be straw mats. These turn out to be roofs for the small shacks belonging to the Rajasthani labourers who live on the other side of an open drain. The walls of these shacks are about four feet high, the rooms about six feet square. There is no sanitation. People use the drain. They bathe at a public tap. During the rains, water moves sluggishly along this drain, but now it is dry except for pools of stagnant, slimy water, a grey liquid tinged with green. It must hold treasures for anyone searching for biological specimens. (And indeed, the enterprising Delhiwala has not ignored this possibility, for farther along, on Link Road, frogs are on sale to biology students.)

At this side of the road lies a dead pony, knocked down at night by a speeding truck. A portion has been eaten away by dogs and jackals. It is now being pecked at by crows; when these birds tire of the stinking carcass they move on to a nearby fruit stall. No one seems to notice this, least of all the fruit vendors. Well-dressed people pass by without a glance at dead horse or open drain. Is it apathy, or is it that Delhi people—city people—are unobservant by nature? Does city life dull the perceptions? Are the giant cinema hoardings so overpowering, so dazzling, that everything else pales into insignificance beside them?

Some of the shack-dwellers have tried to make their homes attractive. They have whitewashed their walls, adorned them with crude but colourful drawings of birds and animals. But what a contrast there is between these humble homes and the elegant villas and bungalows of Kirti Nagar, Patel Road and Pusa Road, three prosperous areas of Delhi which lie on my route. A tenant has to pay anything from three to five hundred rupees a month for a small flat in one of these fine houses.

I went flat-hunting once, but I was turned away by the house-owners—not because of race, colour or religion, but because I was a bachelor. In India, staying single is something of a crime against society. Bachelors have a rough time; they seldom get invited into homes where there are girls of marriageable age.

'Are Delhi bachelors such monsters?' I asked a house agent in Rajinder Nagar.

'Most of them are very well-behaved,' he said. 'But you see, parents no longer have much confidence in their daughters. A girl sees too many films, and then she wants to have a tragic affair with the first good-looking male who comes along.'

It has taken me two hours of foot-slogging to reach Connaught Place, which is still the premier shopping centre of New Delhi, I remember it well from my childhood, in the war years, when my father was stationed at Air Headquarters in New Delhi. The capital was a small, sparsely populated town in those days. We lived in temporary RAF hutments on Wellesley Road. A multi-storeyed hotel now occupies the site. The jungle where I hunted rabbits has long since been cleared to make way for the expensive residential area of Sunder Nagar. But the central vista, leading from India Gate up to Lutyens's complex of Parliament House and the President's Estate, is still a lovely stretch of green grass, still water, and shady jamun trees.

Connaught Place has not changed much. The milk bar I frequented as a boy is still there, although they do not sell milk any more; now it is espresso coffee and hamburgers. The Regal cinema has switched over to Hindi films. In its cellar is a discotheque. Shop-fronts are more flashy, but service-lanes have not altered. And of course the faces and clothes are different. The British uniforms of the war years have given way to the uniforms of the hippies, who slouch about in beads and togas, unaccepted and even scorned by the local citizens. Indians are not impressed by people who do not dress well. Their concept of the true Englishman is of the sahib who dresses for dinner even when there is no dinner; they *like* that kind of Englishman. No one is as clothes-conscious as a Punjabi. He likes his shoes polished, his shirt pressed, his suit spotless—a difficult business in Delhi, where the dust, even in winter, is as thick as in the time of Emperor Shah Jahan who, proud of his new capital, asked the Persian Ambassador how it compared with is Isphahan, and received the double-edged reply: 'By God! Isphahan cannot be compared with the dust of your Delhi!'

But Shah Jahan's Delhi, the old walled city near the Yamuna, is not on my route today. I am tired and hungry, and I lunch at a dhaba, a cheap eating-house, one of many lining the outer pavements round Connaught Place. If one does not mind the filthy surroundings, there is good meat to be had in these little restaurants, most of them run by Punjabis who learned their cooking in Lahore. Certainly the food here is better and cheaper than the watered-down dishes served in some of the smart restaurants in the inner circle. The dish-washers and servers are bare-footed hill boys, working in the city because their small fields in the hills do not provide a sufficient living for their families. They work quite cheerfully (for they are cheerful by nature), in spite of hard words, cuffs, and meagre wages.

Outside, on the road, a small crowd has gathered round a turbaned Pathan. For a moment I fear violence to this exotic stranger; then I realize that the crowd is merely curious, even in good humour. The Pathan is extolling the virtues of an aphrodisiac mixture which he is trying to sell. 'Be happy!' he cries. 'And make your bulbul happy!'

In spite of the family planning hoarding directly behind him, he appears to be doing good business.

It is, after all, the marriage season.

I am forcibly reminded of this on my way home in the evening. The roads in and out of every residential area are blocked by shamianas put up for marriage receptions. This is illegal, but the fine is a small one, and when a father is spending thousands on his daughter's wedding, he dosen't mind paying a fine of forty rupees. He accepts the summons with good humour, and carries on with the reception. This is the month most propitious for marriages. After the 15th of January, four months must pass before a Hindu will marry off his daughter. Astrology plays as great a part in the lives of the people today as it did three hundred years ago when the traveller Francois Bernier observed that no one in Delhi, Hindu or Muslim, undertook any project without first consulting his astrologer. Today, matchmakers must still study the stars in their courses before pairing a boy with a girl.

Most fathers love to give their daughters a good send-off, and Delhi marriages are splendid, glittering affairs. The bridegroom traditionally arrives on a white horse, but Delhiwalas, who like being up-to-date, often use cars, jeeps, or even tractors (because of the high perch they provide).

I find myself involved in a procession on Pusa Road. It is impossible to get past the throng of people, so I must remain with them for some distance. If I choose to attend the reception, no one will turn me away. The bride's people will be under the impression that I am one of the bridegroom's guests, and the bridegroom's group will feel sure that I belong to the bride's party. As most of the guests are seeing each other for the first time, it is possible for any well-dressed person to join the festivities. This frequently happens.

There has, of course, to be a band, and bands are chosen mainly on the strength of the volume of noise they are able to produce and sustain. A trumpet, sounding a foot away from my ear, sends me reeling to the rear of the procession. Drums, bugles, clarinets and saxophones burst into a great profanity of sound. It is not Indian music they play, but an admixture of military marches and popular Hindi film tunes. There is nothing like it anywhere else on earth.

The bandsmen wear red coats and white spats, but shoes are optional. On their heads they wear what appear to be Salvation Army caps. They will play on their instruments (often independently of each other) for as long as they are paid to play, and must deliver a final burst at daybreak when the bride leaves her father's house.

It is a colourful procession, headed by small urchin boys carrying gas lamps. After them comes the band; then the bridegroom's beautifully clothed friends and relatives; and finally the bridegroom, enthroned on top of a gaily caparisoned jeep.

I take a side road and leave the procession, but find my way blocked by another marriage party. This time a heavily-built Sikh, slightly tipsy, embraces me as a long-lost brother. He seems to know me. Quite possibly I knew him when he was a smooth-cheeked lad of fifteen; but now, disguised by a magnificent beard, he reminds me of no one I have ever known. But he wants me to join his party, and so, to humour him, I accompany him for about a hundred yards, when he suddenly forgets me and rushes at some other old acquaintance.

I have to reconnoitre another three processions, and four more shamianas, before I reach Rajouri Garden. I keep going by eating boiled eggs. These are sold on the roadside, and the egg-seller will even peel the egg for you, and serve it sliced, with pepper and salt, on a piece of newspaper. Unfortunately all the egg-sellers disappear when summer comes, because people believe that eggs are 'heating' and should only be eaten during the winter months. I suppose the same reasoning applies to the Pathan's tonic mixture.

I am almost home. It does not look as though anyone in Delhi sleeps at night, but I am ready for bed, and all the brass bands in the city (and there must be over a hundred of them) will not keep me from sleeping.

But there is something I must do first.

The seller of lottery tickets has been staring hopefully at me, and I hate to disappoint him last thing at night. So I produce a rupee and buy a ticket; and, in doing so, I feel that I have finally identified myself with the good people of Delhi.

# Bhabiji's House

*(My neighbours in Rajouri Garden back in the 1960s were the Kamal family. This entry from my journal, which I wrote on one of my later visits, describes a typical day in that household.)*

At first light there is a tremendous burst of birdsong from the guava tree in the little garden. Over a hundred sparrows wake up all at once and give tongue to whatever it is that sparrows have to say to each other at five o'clock on a foggy winter's morning in Delhi.

In the small house, people sleep on; that is, everyone except Bhabiji—Granny—the head of the lively Punjabi middle-class family with whom I nearly always stay when I am in Delhi.

She coughs, stirs, groans, grumbles and gets out of bed. The fire has to be lit, and food prepared for two of her sons to take to work. There is a daughter-in-law, Shobha, to help her; but the girl is not very bright at getting up in the morning. Actually, it is this way: Bhabiji wants to show up her daughter-in-law; so, no matter how hard Shobha tries to be up first, Bhabiji forestalls her. The old lady does not sleep well, anyway; her eyes are open long before the first sparrow chirps, and as soon as she sees her daughter-in-law stirring, she scrambles out of bed and hurries to the kitchen. This gives her the opportunity to say: 'What good is a daughter-in-law when I have to get up to prepare her husband's food?'

The truth is that Bhabiji does not like anyone else preparing her sons' food.

She looks no older than when I first saw her ten years ago. She still has complete control over a large family and, with tremendous confidence and enthusiasm, presides over the lives of three sons, a daughter, two daughters-in-law and fourteen grandchildren. This is a joint family (there are not many left in a big city like Delhi), in which the sons and their families all live together as one unit under their mother's benevolent (and sometimes slightly malevolent) autocracy. Even when her husband was alive, Bhabiji dominated the household.

The eldest son, Shiv, has a separate kitchen, but his wife and children participate in all the family celebrations and quarrels. It is a small miracle how everyone (including myself when I visit) manages to fit into the house; and a stranger might be forgiven for wondering where everyone sleeps, for no beds are visible during the day. That is because the beds—light wooden frames with rough string across—are brought in only at night, and are taken out first thing in the morning and kept in the garden shed.

As Bhabiji lights the kitchen fire, the household begins to stir, and Shobha joins her mother-in-law in the kitchen. As a guest I am privileged and may get up last. But my bed soon becomes an island battered by waves of scurrying, shouting children, eager to bathe, dress, eat and find their school books. Before I can get up, someone brings me a tumbler of hot sweet tea. It is a brass tumbler and burns my fingers; I have yet to learn how to hold one properly. Punjabis like their tea with lots of milk and sugar—so much so that I often wonder why they bother to add any tea.

Ten years ago, 'bed tea' was unheard of in Bhabiji's

house. Then, the first time I came to stay, Kamal, the youngest son, told Bhabiji: 'My friend is *Angrez*. He must have tea in bed.' He forgot to mention that I usually took my morning cup at seven; they gave it to me at five. I gulped it down and went to sleep again. Then, slowly, others in the household began indulging in morning cups of tea. Now everyone, including the older children, has 'bed tea'. They bless my English forebears for instituting the custom; I bless the Punjabis for perpetuating it.

Breakfast is by rota, in the kitchen. It is a tiny room and accommodates only four adults at a time. The children have eaten first; but the smallest children, Shobha's toddlers, keep coming in and climbing over us. Says Bhabiji of the youngest and most mischievous: 'He lives only because God keeps a special eye on him.'

Kamal, his elder brother Arun and I sit cross-legged and barefooted on the floor while Bhabiji serves us hot parathas stuffed with potatoes and onions, along with omelettes, an excellent dish. Arun then goes to work on his scooter, while Kamal catches a bus for the city, where he attends an art college. After they have gone, Bhabiji and Shobha have their breakfast.

By nine o'clock everyone who is still in the house is busy doing something. Shobha is washing clothes. Bhabiji has settled down on a cot with a huge pile of spinach, which she methodically cleans and chops up. Madhu, her fourteen-year-old granddaughter, who attends school only in the afternoons, is washing down the sitting room floor. Madhu's mother is a teacher in a primary school in Delhi, and earns a pittance of Rs 150 a month. Her husband went to England ten years ago, and never returned; he does not send any money home.

Madhu is made attractive by the gravity of her countenance. She is always thoughtful, reflective; seldom speaks, smiles rarely (but looks very pretty when she does). I wonder what she thinks about as she scrubs floors, prepares meals with Bhabiji, washes dishes and even finds a few hard-pressed moments for her school work. She is the Cinderella of the house. Not that she has to put up with anything like a cruel stepmother. Madhu is Bhabiji's favourite. She has made herself so useful that she is above all reproach. Apart from that, there is a certain measure of aloofness about her—she does not get involved in domestic squabbles—and this is foreign to a household in which everyone has something to say for himself or herself. Her two young brothers are constantly being reprimanded; but no one says anything to Madhu. Only yesterday morning, when clothes were being washed and Madhu was scrubbing the floor, the following dialogue took place.

Madhu's mother (picking up a school book left in the courtyard): 'Where's that boy Popat? See how careless he is with his books! Popat! He's run off. Just wait till he gets back. I'll give him a good beating.'

Vinod's mother: 'It's not Popat's book. It's Vinod's. Where's Vinod?'

Vinod (grumpily): 'It's Madhu's book.'

Silence for a minute or two. Madhu continues scrubbing the floor; she does not bother to look up. Vinod picks up the book and takes it indoors. The women return to their chores.

Manju, daughter of Shiv and sister of Vinod, is averse to housework and, as a result, is always being scolded—by her parents, grandmother, uncles and aunts.

Now, she is engaged in the unwelcome chore of sweeping the front yard. She does this with a sulky look, ignoring my cheerful remarks. I have been sitting under the guava tree, but Manju soon sweeps me away from this spot. She creates a drifting cloud of dust, and seems satisfied only when the dust settles on the clothes that have just been hung up to dry. Manju is a sensuous creature and, like most sensuous people, is lazy by nature. She does not like sweeping because the boy next door can see her at it, and she wants to appear before him in a more glamorous light. Her first action every morning is to turn to the cinema advertisements in the newspaper. Bombay's movie moguls cater for girls like Manju who long to be tragic heroines. Life is so very dull for middle-class teenagers in Delhi that it is only natural that they should lean so heavily on escapist entertainment. Every residential area has a cinema. But there is not a single bookshop in this particular suburb, although it has a population of over twenty thousand literate people. Few children read books; but they are adept at swotting up examination 'guides'; and students of, say, Hardy or Dickens read the guides and not the novels.

Bhabiji is now grinding onions and chillies in a mortar. Her eyes are watering but she is in a good mood. Shobha sits quietly in the kitchen. A little while ago she was complaining to me of a backache. I am the only one who lends a sympathetic ear to complaints of aches and pains. But since last night, my sympathies have been under severe strain. When I got into bed at about ten o'clock, I found the sheets wet. Apparently Shobha had put her baby to sleep in my bed during the afternoon.

While the housework is still in progress, cousin Kishore arrives. He is an itinerant musician who makes a living by arranging performances at marriages. He visits Bhabiji's house frequently and at odd hours, often a little tipsy, always brimming over with goodwill and grandiose plans for the future. It was once his ambition to be a film producer, and some years back he lost a lot of Bhabiji's money in producing a film that was never completed. He still talks of finishing it.

'Brother,' he says, taking me into his confidence for the hundredth time, 'do you know anyone who has a movie camera?'

'No,' I say, knowing only too well how these admissions can lead me into a morass of complicated manoeuvres. But Kishore is not easily put off, especially when he has been fortified with country liquor.

'But you *knew* someone with a movie camera?' He asks.

'That was long ago.'

'How long ago?' (I have got him going now.)

'About five years back.'

'Only five years? Find him, find him!'

'It's no use. He doesn't have the movie camera any more. He sold it.'

'Sold it!' Kishore looks at me as though I have done him an injury. 'But why didn't you buy it? All we need is a movie camera, and our fortune is made. I will produce the film, I will direct it, I will write the music. Two in one, Charlie Chaplin and Raj Kapoor. Why didn't you buy the camera?'

'Because I didn't have the money.'

'But we could have borrowed the money.'

'If you are in a position to borrow money, you can go out and buy another movie camera.'

'We could have borrowed the camera. Do you know anyone else who has one?'

'Not a soul.' I am firm this time; I will not be led into another maze.

'Very sad, very sad,' mutters Kishore. And with a dejected, hang-dog expression designed to make me feel that I am responsible for all his failures, he moves off.

Bhabiji had expressed some annoyance at his arrival, but he softens her up by leaving behind an invitation to a marriage party this evening. No one in the house knows the bride's or bridegroom's family, but that does not matter; knowing one of the musicians is just as good. Almost everyone will go.

While Bhabiji, Shobha and Madhu are preparing lunch, Bhabiji engages in one of her favourite subjects of conversation, Kamal's marriage, which she hopes she will be able to arrange in the near future. She freely acknowledges that she made grave blunders in selecting wives for her other sons—this is meant to be heard by Shobha—and promises not to repeat her mistakes. According to Bhabiji, Kamal's bride should be both educated and domesticated; and of course she must be fair.

'What if he likes a dark girl?' I ask teasingly.

Bhabiji looks horrified. 'He cannot marry a dark girl,' she declares.

'But dark girls are beautiful,' I tell her.

'Impossible!'

'Do you want him to marry a European girl?'

'No foreigners! I know them, they'll take my son away. He shall have a good Punjabi girl, with a complexion the colour of wheat.'

Noon. The shadows shift and cross the road. I sit beneath the guava tree and watch the women at work. They will not let me do anything, but they like talking to me and they love to hear my broken Punjabi. Sparrows flit about at their feet, snapping up the grain that runs away from their busy fingers. A crow looks speculatively at the empty kitchen, sidles towards the open door; but Bhabiji has only to glance up and the experienced crow flies away. He knows he will not be able to make off with anything from this house.

One by one the children come home, demanding food. Now it is Madhu's turn to go to school. Her younger brother Popat, an intelligent but undersized boy of thirteen, appears in the doorway and asks for lunch.

'Be off!' says Bhabiji. 'It isn't ready yet.'

Actually the food is ready and only the chapatis remain to be made. Shobha will attend to them. Bhabiji lies down on her cot in the sun, complaining of a pain in her back and ringing noises in her ears.

'I'll press your back,' says Popat. He has been out of Bhabiji's favour lately, and is looking for an opportunity to be rehabilitated.

Barefooted he stands on Bhabiji's back and treads her weary flesh and bones with a gentle walking-in-one-spot movement. Bhabiji grunts with relief. Every day she has new pains in new places. Her age, and the daily business of feeding the family and running everyone's affairs, are beginning to tell on her. But she would sooner die than give up her position of dominance in the house. Her working sons still hand over their pay to her, and she dispenses the money as she sees fit.

The pummelling she gets from Popat puts her in a better mood, and she holds forth on another favourite subject, the respective merits of various dowries. Shiv's wife (according to Bhabiji) brought nothing with her but a string cot; Kishore's wife brought only a sharp and clever tongue; Shobha brought a wonderful steel cupboard, fully expecting that it would do all the housework for her.

This last observation upsets Shobha, and a little later I find her under the guava tree, weeping profusely. I give her the comforting words she obviously expects; but it is her husband Arun who will have to bear the brunt of her outraged feelings when he comes home this evening. He is rather nervous of his wife. Last night he wanted to eat out, at a restaurant, but did not want to be accused of wasting money; so he stuffed fifteen rupees into my pocket and asked me to invite both him and Shobha to dinner, which I did. We had a good dinner. Such unexpected hospitality on my part has further improved my standing with Shobha. Now, in spite of other chores, she sees that I get cups of tea and coffee at odd hours of the day.

Bhabiji knows Arun is soft with his wife, and taunts him about it. She was saying this morning that whenever there is any work to be done Shobha retires to bed with a headache (partly true). She says even Manju does more housework (not true). Bhabiji has certain talents as an actress, and does a good take-off of Shobha sulking and grumbling at having too much to do.

While Bhabiji talks, Popat sneaks off and goes for

a ride on the bicycle. It is a very old bicycle and is constantly undergoing repairs. 'The soul has gone out of it,' says Vinod philosophically and makes his way on to the roof, where he keeps a store of pornographic literature. Up there, he cannot be seen and cannot be remembered, and so avoids being sent out on errands.

One of the boys is bathing at the hand-pump. Manju, who should have gone to school with Madhu, is stretched out on a cot, complaining of fever. But she will be up in time to attend the marriage party. . .

Towards evening, as the birds return to roost in the guava tree, their chatter is challenged by the tumult of people in the house getting ready for the marriage party.

Manju presses her tight pyjamas but neglects to darn them. She wears a loose-fitting, diaphanous shirt. She keeps flitting in and out of the front room so that I can admire the way she glitters. Shobha has used too much powder and lipstick in an effort to look like the femme fatale which she indubitably is not. Shiv's more conservative wife floats around in loose, old-fashioned pyjamas. Bhabiji is sober and austere in a white sari. Madhu looks neat. The men wear their suits.

Popat is holding up a mirror for his Uncle Kishore, who is combing his long hair. (Kishore kept his hair long, like a court musician at the time of Akbar, before the hippies had been heard of.) He is nodding benevolently, having fortified himself from a bottle labelled 'Som Ras' ('Nectar of the Gods'), obtained cheaply from an illicit still.

Kishore: 'Don't shake the mirror, boy!'

Popat: 'Uncle, it's your head that's shaking.'

Shobha is happy. She loves going out, especially

to marriages, and she always takes her two small boys with her, although they invariably spoil the carpets.

Only Kamal, Popat and I remain behind. I have had more than my share of marriage parties.

The house is strangely quiet. It does not seem so small now, with only three people left in it. The kitchen has been locked (Bhabiji will not leave it open while Popat is still in the house), so we visit the dhaba, the wayside restaurant near the main road, and this time I pay the bill with my own money. We have kababs and chicken curry.

Yesterday Kamal and I took our lunch on the grass of the Buddha Jayanti Gardens (Buddha's Birthday Gardens). There was no college for Kamal, as the majority of Delhi's students had hijacked a number of corporation buses and headed for the Pakistan High Commission, with every intention of levelling it to the ground if possible, as a protest against the hijacking of an Indian plane from Srinagar to Lahore. The students were met by the Delhi police in full strength, and a pitched battle took place, in which stones from the students and tear gas shells from the police were the favoured missiles. There were two shells fired every minute, according to a newspaper report. And this went on all day. A number of students and policemen were injured, but by some miracle no one was killed. The police held their ground, and the Pakistan High Commission remained inviolate. But the Australian High Commission, situated to the rear of the student brigade, received most of the tear gas shells, and had to close down for the day.

Kamal and I attended the siege for about an hour, before retiring to the Gardens with our ham sandwiches. A couple of friendly squirrels came up to investigate, and were soon taking bread from our hands. We could hear the chanting of the students in the distance. I lay back on the grass and opened my copy of *Barchester Towers*. Whenever life in Delhi, or in Bhabiji's house (or anywhere, for that matter), becomes too tumultuous, I turn to Trollope. Nothing could be further removed from the turmoil of our times than an English cathedral town in the nineteenth century. But I think Jane Austen would have appreciated life in Bhabiji's house.

By ten o'clock, everyone is back from the marriage. (They had gone for the feast, and not for the ceremonies, which continue into the early hours of the morning.) Shobha is full of praise for the bridegroom's good looks and fair complexion. She describes him as being *'gora-chitta'*—very white! She does not have a high opinion of the bride.

Shiv, in a happy and reflective mood, extols the qualities of his own wife, referring to her as The Barrel. He tells us how, shortly after their marriage, she had threatened to throw a brick at the next-door girl. This little incident remains fresh in Shiv's mind, after eighteen years of marriage.

He says: 'When the neighbours came and complained, I told them, "It is quite possible that my wife will throw a brick at your daughter. She is in the habit of throwing bricks." The neighbours held their peace.'

I think Shiv is rather proud of his wife's militancy when it comes to taking on neighbours; recently she vanquished the woman next door (a formidable Sikh lady) after a verbal battle that lasted three hours. But in arguments or quarrels with Bhabiji, Shiv's wife always loses, because Shiv takes his mother's side.

Arun, on the other hand, is afraid of both wife and mother, and simply makes himself scarce when a quarrel develops. Or he tells his mother she is right, and then, to placate Shobha, takes her to the pictures.

Kishore turns up just as everyone is about to go to bed. Bhabiji is annoyed at first, because he has been drinking too much; but when he produces a bunch of cinema tickets, she is mollified and asks him to stay the night. Not even Bhabiji likes missing a new picture.

Kishore is urging me to write his life story.

'Your life would make a most interesting story,' I tell him. 'But it will be interesting only if I put in everything—your successes *and* your failures.'

'No, no, only successes,' exhorts Kishore. 'I want you to describe me as a popular music director.'

'But you have yet to become popular.'

'I will be popular if you write about me.'

Fortunately we are interrupted by the cots being brought in. Then Bhabiji and Shiv go into a huddle, discussing plans for building an extra room. After all, Kamal may be married soon.

One by one, the children get under their quilts. Popat starts massaging Bhabiji's back. She gives him her favourite blessing: 'God protect you and give you lots of children.' If God listens to all Bhabiji's prayers and blessings, there will never be a fall in the population.

The lights are off and Bhabiji settles down for the night. She is almost asleep when a small voice pipes up: 'Bhabiji, tell us a story'

At first Bhabiji pretends not to hear; then, when the request is repeated, she says: 'You'll keep Aunty Shobha awake, and then she'll have an excuse for getting up late in the morning.' But the children know

Bhabiji's one great weakness, and they renew their demand.

'Your grandmother is tired,' says Arun. 'Let her sleep.'

But Bhabiji's eyes are open. Her mind is going back over the crowded years, and she remembers something very interesting that happened when her younger brother's wife's sister married the eldest son of her third cousin. . .

Before long, the children are asleep, and I am wondering if I will ever sleep, for Bhabiji's voice drones on, into the darker reaches of the night.

# Break of the Monsoon

From Delhi I made occasional forays into nearby towns. Meerut was one of the towns I travelled to, and there, one evening, I saw the magic of the monsoon.

I was staying at a small hotel. There had been no rain for a month, but the atmosphere was humid, there were clouds overhead, dark clouds burgeoning with moisture. Thunder blossomed in the air.

The monsoon was going to break that day. I knew it; the birds knew it; the grass knew it. There was the smell of rain in the air. And the grass, the birds and I responded to this odour with the same sensuous longing.

A large drop of water hit the windowsill, darkening the thick dust on the woodwork. A faint breeze had sprung up, and again I felt the moisture, closer and warmer.

Then the rain approached like a dark curtain.

I could see it marching down the street, heavy and remorseless. It drummed on the corrugated tin roof and swept across the road and over the balcony of my room. I sat there without moving, letting the rain soak my sticky shirt and gritty hair.

Outside, the street rapidly emptied. The crowd dissolved in the rain. Then buses, cars and bullock-carts ploughed through the suddenly rushing water. A group of small boys, gloriously naked, came romping along a side street, which was like a river in spate. A garland of marigolds, swept off the steps of a temple, came floating down the middle of the road.

The rain stopped as suddenly as it had begun. The day was dying, and the breeze remained cool and moist. In the brief twilight that followed, I was witness to the great yearly flight of insects into the cool brief freedom of the night.

Termites and white ants, which had been sleeping through the hot season, emerged from their lairs. Out of every hole and crack, and from under the roots of trees, huge winged ants emerged, fluttering about heavily on this, the first and last flight of their lives. There was only one direction in which they could fly — towards the light, towards the street lights and the bright neon tubelight above my balcony.

The light above the balcony attracted a massive, quivering swarm of clumsy termites, giving the impression of one thick, slowly revolving mass. A frog had found its way through the bathroom and came hopping across the balcony to pause beneath the light. All he had to do was gobble, as insects fell around him.

This was the hour of the geckos, the wall lizards. They had their reward for weeks of patient waiting. Plying their sticky pink tongues, they devoured insects as swiftly and methodically as children devour popcorn. For hours they crammed their stomachs, knowing that such a feast would not come their way again. Throughout the entire hot season the insect world had prepared for this flight out of darkness into light, and the phenomenon would not happen again for another year.

In hot up-country towns in India it is good to have the first monsoon showers arrive at night, while you are sleeping on the veranda. You wake up to the scent of wet earth and fallen neem leaves, and find that a hot and stuffy bungalow has been converted into a cool, damp place. The swish of the banana fronds and the drumming of the rain on broad-leaved sal trees will soothe the most fevered brow.

During the rains the frogs have a perfect Country Music Festival. There are two sets of them, it seems, and they sing antiphonal chants all evening, each group letting the other take its turn in the fairest manner. No one sees or hears them during the hot weather, but the moment the monsoon breaks they swarm all over the place.

When night comes on, great moths fly past, and beetles of all shapes and sizes come whirring in at the open windows. Recently, when Prem closed my window to keep out these winged visitors, I remonstrated, saying that as a nature lover I would share my room with them. I'd forgotten that I am inclined to sleep with my mouth open. In the wee hours I woke up, spluttering and choking, to find that I had almost swallowed a large and somewhat unpleasant-tasting moth. I closed the window. Moths are lovely creatures, but a good night's sleep is even lovelier.

At night the fireflies light up their lamps, flashing messages to each other through the mango groves. Some nocturnal insects thrive mainly at the expense of humans. Sometimes one wakes up to find thirty or forty mosquitoes looking through the netting in a bloodthirsty manner. If you are sleeping out, you will need that mosquito netting.

The road outside is lined with fine babul trees, now covered with powdery little balls of yellow blossom, filling the air with a faint scent. After the first showers there is a great deal of water about, and for many miles the trees are standing in it. The common monsoon sights along an up-country road are often picturesque—the wide plains, with great herds of smoke-coloured, delicate-limbed cattle being driven slowly home for the night, accompanied by troops of ungainly buffaloes and flocks of black long-tailed sheep. Then you come to a pond, where the buffaloes are indulging in a sensuous wallow, no part of them visible but the tips of their noses.

Within a few days of the first rain the air is full of dragonflies, crossing and re-crossing, poised motionless for a moment, then darting away with that mingled grace and power which is unmatched among insects. Dragonflies are the swallows of the insect world; their prey is the mosquito, the gnat, the midge and the fly. These swarms, therefore, tell us that the moistened surface of the ground, with its mouldering leaves and sodden grass, has become one vast incubator teeming with every form of ephemeral life.

After the monotony of a fierce sun and a dusty landscape quivering in the dim distance, one welcomes these days of mild light, green earth, and purple hills coming nearer in the clear and transparent air.

And later on, when the monsoon begins to break up and the hills are dappled with light and shade, dark islands of cloud moving across the bright green sea, the effect on one's spirits is strangely exhilarating.

# II

## TALES OF THE OPEN ROAD

# On the Highway

Once or twice a year, in self-indulgent mood, I give myself a 'treat', if you can call it that: a seven-hour drive to Delhi from Mussoorie, in an old but sturdy Ambassador taxi. Winter is the best time for such a visit. The hot winds of summer are best avoided, for once you have descended from the hills, the road becomes dusty, and in places something of an obstacle race.

I have known this highway over the years and I have seen it change imperceptibly. There wasn't much traffic on it in the 1940s, apart from the familiar bullock-carts stacked high with sugar cane. The carts are still used, although the wooden wheels have given way to heavy tyres, and the bullocks to buffaloes. Most of the cane is now carried in trucks, and these 'kings of the road' have made it difficult for others to drive smoothly by day or safely by night. The trucks and the sugar cane keep the economy going, so we shouldn't grumble too much. This is one of the wealthiest agricultural areas in the land—Shamli, in its heartland, has the highest per capita income in the country, according to my bank manager—and from field to factory, and factory to town, the truckers are the ones to do the job.

Shamli is not one of the places you normally pass through on the way to Delhi. Not unless you are the actor Tom Alter and your driver takes the wrong turning in the middle of the night.

Tom got into his favourite Mussoorie taxi, leaving town after dinner as he had to be in Delhi early next morning. The driver fortified himself with a couple of drinks while Tom, who doesn't drink, settled into the back seat for a nap. He woke up to find himself in Shamli instead of Roorkee; but they eventually returned to the main highway and, having completed half the journey, the driver felt the need for further refreshment and stopped at a wayside inn where he fell in with some of his buddies. Tom got out of the car to stretch his legs. He crossed the road and gazed out across the moonlit mustard fields. When he turned back to the taxi, he found it had vanished! The inebriated driver had returned to the wheel and, without glancing back to see if his passenger was still in the back seat, had driven on. An hour later, on reaching the outskirts of Meerut, the driver discovered that Tom was missing. Crestfallen, he was about to turn back in search of his lost passenger when Tom himself arrived, having hitched a ride on an early-morning milk van.

Although I have been up and down the Delhi road two or three times a year, for the last forty years, I have been fortunate in that I have experienced relatively few mishaps. And when my nature-loving bank manager, Vishal Ohri, decided to give me a treat some years ago by taking a short cut from Hardwar through the Rajaji Sanctuary and out at the Mohand Pass, I did not demur. I'm the ideal front-seat passenger, as I cannot drive and simply put my faith in God and the travelling public in general. Vishal Ohri enjoys his driving, especially in rough conditions; unfortunately his ancient Fiat was in poor condition, and half-way through the Sanctuary, while we were crossing a boulder-strewn *rao* (a semi-dry riverbed) the door on my side fell off and I very nearly went with it. For the rest of the journey, I had an uninterrupted view of the wildlife in the sanctuary—two peahens, a startled porcupine, and a herd of tame buffaloes.

\* \* \*

Driving by night is not always so risible. Most accidents on the main highway road occur in the early hours when drivers fall asleep at the wheel: their vehicles overturn, or run into trees and ditches, or collide with other vehicles. Before dawn breaks, the road has taken its toll of several lives.

It was late Christmas Eve in the 1970s, when my thirty-year-old half-brother Harold set out from Dehra in his father's car, to try and get to Delhi in time for a party at the Anglo-Indian Club. Although he was a good driver, having taken part in car rallies and other tests of speed and endurance, he had become a heavy drinker and he was in no condition to undertake a long and arduous drive late at night. He was alone, and as he was killed instantly (or so it appeared), we never knew all the circumstances of the accident. Apparently his car had been caught and crushed between two trucks, which had speedily disappeared into the night.

What can one say about Harold? He was attractive to women, but they had a hard time looking after him. And he wrecked their lives in addition to his own.

Harold's interests and mine were very different, but we did not get in each other's way. He left me to my books and long walks; I left him to his motorcycles and dance parties. Our mother indulged him; his father left him to his own devices.

53

Our mother died a year or two before Harold's fatal accident, and so she was spared a lot of heartbreak— double heartbreak, because a few months later my second half-brother died in a motorcycle accident. He was the careful one, who seldom took risks, so I don't suppose there are any lessons to be learnt.

\* \* \*

I haven't driven through Meerut for many years, because most cars now take the bypass. Back in the 1960s it would provide an escape from Delhi, and I would spend an occasional weekend there, staying with old Captain Saulez in the cantonment and attending the Meerut races. The Meerut races were always a shade superior to the Delhi races, as they were patronized by the Army. Captain Saulez, a legendary racehorse owner and trainer, was a familiar figure in Meerut, moving about in his little pony-trap. His daughter had married a Swiss journalist, William Matheson, much disliked by the Captain. It was at William's invitation that I first went to stay at their bungalow in its sprawling grounds on Centre Road. The Captain paid no attention to me. This meant he approved of me, according to William; most other visitors weren't allowed in at the gate. On summer nights I slept out of doors, kept awake for long hours by a brain-fever bird screaming at me from a gulmohur tree. There were many trees in the compound, as well as lots of open space for the horses to exercise.

Captain Saulez died many years ago, mourned by jockeys and racing people if not by his relatives. William and his wife left the country. I wonder if the house and grounds have gone too, swallowed up by the march of time and the pressures of population. It is unlikely that I will go that way again. It is good to remember the past, but to return to places associated with one's youth can often be disappointing. An old school friend of mine visited Saharanpur after fifty years, hoping to find the house where he had grown up. Instead he found a crowded bus stand. And in Delhi, the bungalow and garden where I spent a year or two of my childhood has vanished and in its place has risen a massive high-rise building, with hundreds of cars parked where sweet peas and roses once flourished.

'You may break, you may shatter the vase if you will,
But the scent of the roses will linger there still. . .'

* * *

The byways of history have always fascinated me. The history books tell us about Delhi, Calcutta, Madras and Bombay, but they have little to say about the drama that takes place in the lives of those living in villages or small towns. There are stories to be told about all these places.

While living in Delhi in the early 1960s, I made a number of excursions to small and large towns in the Hindi heartland—Agra, Mathura, Rishikesh, Aligarh, Shahjahanpur . . .

In Shahjahanpur I located the church and compound where the tragic incidents of the 1857 uprising occurred. My novella, *A Flight of Pigeons*, was based on the actual experiences of Ruth Labadoor, a fourteen-year-old Anglo-Indian girl who survived the massacre.*

The pieces that follow are extracted from the journal I kept at the time.

---

* The novella is included in my book *Our Trees Still Grow in Dehra*.

# Rishikesh

*'Ganga mai ki jai!'* (May mother Ganga flow for ever!)

Everyone raised the cry as the Hardwar bus moved out of Meerut. Most of the passengers, including Kamal and I, were going to take *darshan* of Mother Ganga. But while many were bound for Hardwar, we were going to Rishikesh, a more secluded temple-town, situated on the banks of the Ganga at the point where the river emerges from the mountains and, hemmed in no longer by rocks and trees, stretches itself across the plains of Uttar Pradesh and Bihar, flowing past great cities like Kanpur, Allahabad, Benares and Patna, and into Bengal.

Just next to us sat a well-built woman with three small children. The eldest, a boy of about six, took a fancy to Kamal, and was soon lolling about on his knees. In front of us, obliterating the view, sat a stout 'lala' and his devoted wife. Lalaji proved to be an impatient and ill-tempered man. He quarrelled with the conductor, the driver and the ticket-seller. In order to travel in comfort he had reserved three front seats, but was unwilling to pay toll on the third seat which, he insisted, would only be occupied by his and his wife's feet. They gave in to him eventually. An urchin who inadvertently touched the sleeve of his kurta received a stinging slap. But he became more tolerant as time went on, and once, when engaged in an argument with a passenger at the other end of the bus, favoured me with a smile.

The countryside was monotonous up to Roorkee.

Then the road took us along the Ganga canal, and Kamal sat up and began to look at things. We changed buses at Hardwar, and got into a very old and wheezy contraption which surprised us by going much faster than the government roadways bus. Probably the driver was trying to make up for time lost in stopping every five minutes to pick up some acquaintance on the road. We stopped for ten minutes at the Sat Narain temple, once famous for the tiger that used to visit it every evening. Rattling through the Motichur forest block, we saw two elephants—tame ones, possibly— and a variety of monkeys.

We left the bus at Rishikesh and went in search of my friend Jhardari, with whom we were to stay. He lived at Muni-ki-Reti, two miles upstream, where the wealthier ashrams were situated. His rooms, adjoining Swami Sivananda's Ashram, were on the right-hand bank of the Ganga.

Jhardhari was away, on a routine trip to Devprayag. As Secretary of the Tehri-Garhwal Motor Mazdoor Sangh Workers' Union, he has to travel all over the district to keep in touch with the men who drive the trucks and buses on the dangerous hill roads. The buses are privately owned, the government only nationalizes those services that use first-class roads. The state is very cautious about taking over the responsibility of transporting people to remote hill towns like Tehri and Pipalkoti, where pilgrims on the way to Gangotri or Badrinath must start their journey on foot. The motor roads in the interior are narrow, precipitous and unmetalled. To mention this is not to condemn them. Till a few years ago many of these regions had no roads at all. And Garhwalis are excellent drivers—many have experience of Army trucks—and serious accidents are uncommon.

Jhardhari's room-mate made us at home, and prepared hot, strong tea. Garhwalis drink more tea than Englishmen, and seldom take water. We were to become accustomed to drinking tea at almost hourly intervals.

One of the first things we did was to dip ourselves in the river. The water was icy cold, and it was impossible to stay in for more than ten minutes. Shivering, we climbed on to the bathing steps to dry ourselves. Our clothes felt hot against our bodies.

Down at the Rishikesh bathing ghat, hundreds of people would be dipping themselves in the sacred waters; but at Muni-ki-reti (which is in Tehri-Garhwal district, while the town of Rishikesh is in Dehra Dun district) there were only a few people by the river—a few pilgrims from Bengal, Andhra and Madras; disciples from Swami Sivananda's Ashram; and a number of boys who work in the area.

Logs were always floating downstream, and boys would get across them, lying flat on their stomachs and paddling the planks through the water. Two of the more daring youths paddled their logs right across the river, to the temples on the opposite bank. They were good swimmers, but had they been parted from their floats they would have been carried away by the current and quite possibly drowned.

We walked down to Rishikesh in the evening, and saw over a hundred sadhus emerging from an ashram where they were given their evening meal. In their saffron robes, they flooded the dusty road, talking animatedly amongst themselves. Many of them were young men, probably novices. One was a strapping youth of about twenty, a Hercules gracefully wearing the robe of renunciation.

They looked well-fed and contented. Most of them spoke a little English. What had brought them to Rishikesh, I wondered, to live as recluses and ascetics? Personal tragedy, the stress of modern city life, or the failure of material pursuits. . . Or did the career of a religious mendicant hold out profitable prospects? Later on I was told that some of the novitiates should really have been in prison. But perhaps the rigours of their monastic existence rid them of early criminal tendencies; and if that was so, then surely ashrams were better places for them than jails.

Little shacks lined the river banks and though few people bathed late in the evening, hundreds were beside the water. Offerings of flowers in little leaf boats went sailing downstream. They were lighted by wicks dipped in oil, and went bobbing up and down on the water, sometimes for a considerable distance, until they were upset by rocks or inquisitive fish. Kamal sent an offering downstream, and requested Mother Ganga to grant him success as an artist. His boat, though, did not go very far. It came between the legs of a bather, an enormous Amazonian woman, and disappeared beneath her.

Undeterred, Kamal fed little balls of flour to the fish. They were huge, completely tame, and came to the bank in shoals to be fed by the bathers. Sometimes they fought amongst themselves, and a few of them were a raw pink where they had been savagely bitten.

That night we slept in the open, on a wide ledge above the riverbed. The lights from the temples and ashrams on the opposite bank reflected gently on the water. There was a *human* quietness everywhere. The sounds were of the river—the distant roar of the rapids, the nearby lapping of water on the bathing steps.

* * *

We bathed again in the river, as the sun came up over the mountain known as Manikoot Parbat. There is an unbroken ridge along the top of this mountain, stretching all the way to the snows of Badrinath, some two hundred miles away. Only a few hermits live on the mountain. It belongs to the elephants who sometimes visit the river in herds, to bathe and drink.

Jhardhari had returned, looking quite fresh after a 150-mile bus journey; and he offered to take us up to Narindernagar, a little town on a hilltop, which, though smaller and less central than Tehri, is the capital of the district. The former Maharaja had preferred it to the less congenial valley-town of Tehri on the banks of the Bhagirathi; and Narindernagar became the Maharaja's summer capital.

The buses were all full, and we had to travel up separately, one to each bus. First Kamal, then I, and last of all Jhardhari.

Narindernagar is only ten miles from Rishikesh, but it is also two thousand feet higher, and the bus has to climb a dizzy, winding road on which there can be no two-way traffic. But the buses go faster than their counterparts in the plains. With speedometers conveniently out of order, buses and trucks come downhill at a speed of thirty to thirty-five miles an hour. But, as I have said before, Garhwalis are very good drivers. Along the main highways of the Punjab are the wrecks of numerous trucks, some jammed up against trees, others in head-on collisions. But in the hills there is no driving at night, and the drivers prefer smoking bidis to drinking rum or country liquor. Mechanical failure is usually the cause of the few accidents that do occur.

From Narindernagar we went on for another eight miles, and eventually got down at Agra-khal, a pass in the mountains at a height of about five thousand feet. The motor road, soon becoming kaccha, continues to Tehri and Dharasu, and from the latter, pilgrims must proceed on foot to the shrines and temples of Gangotri.

After eating some hot puris, we walked back to Narindernagar, leaving the main road, and hiking through a forest of oak and pine. Kamal, who was seeing real mountains for the first time, was very excited and asked me innumerable questions about plants and streams and trees and rocks. He chattered away until Jhardhari said something flattering about his many and varied interests, and this embarrassed Kamal so much that he stopped talking altogether. I enjoyed the shade of the gnarled, untidy oaks, and the soft, slippery carpet of pine needles.

But after the forest there was bare hillside, the sun was scorching hot, and we had soon emptied the water bottle. So we rejoined the main road and stopped a truck going down to Rishikesh.

It was the first time Kamal and I had sat in the back of a truck travelling at speed down a mountain. It was impossible to anchor oneself on the floor. A kindly sadhu, also at the back, placed his blanket on a tyre and invited us to share it with him; but at every hairpin bend the tyre slid violently about the floor and we were pitched off it. Kamal and I clung to each other to avoid being thrown against the sides of the truck; Jhardhari hung on to an iron bar; we were all feeling quite sick. Only the sadhu appeared unperturbed. He retained his seat on the tyre, even when it went skidding from one end of the truck to the other.

When we reached Rishikesh we went straight to the river. Never had Mother Ganga's waters been so refreshing. The giddiness disappeared. Then we lay down on the sand, and Kamal, like the sleepy giant Kumbhakarna in the *Ramayana*, did not come to life until it was time to eat.

We slept well that night. In the morning we would go to Lachhman Jhula and, passing the suspension bridge, walk a little way up Manikoot Parbat.

\*\*\*

As the sun rose, turning the river to gold, we climbed into the boat that took pilgrims across to the temples on the other bank. The oarsmen sat in the prow, straining against the current, and the people in the boat raised the same ageless cry: '*Ganga Mai ki jai!*'

Climbing ashore, we passed through groves of mango trees, planted by rich pilgrims for the benefit of the sadhus. Then, leaving behind Lachhman Jhula, we walked along the pilgrim route to Badrinath until we came to a dharamshala called Garur Chatti. Here we drank tea, the inevitable but welcome tea, and set off up the hillside in search of a waterfall Jhardhari had told us about.

It did not take us long to reach the waterfall. Set amidst rocks and ferns, it fell about thirty feet onto a platform of smooth yellow rocks and pebbles. Here it formed a small pool, about waist deep, into which we leapt without hesitation. The water wasn't as cold as the Ganga's, and we could splash about for as long as we liked, while the waterfall sprayed down on our heads. The water was very clear and fresh, though it had a slightly bitter taste, evidence, I suppose, of a strong mineral content.

Further down the stream we found a lot of old bones, which Kamal insisted were the remains of a tiger's kill; as, indeed, they might have been, tigers having been seen on the mountain. But no tiger troubled us; only a band of langurs, swinging from tree to tree, seemed resentful of our presence and urged us to leave.

This we did at our leisure and, after more tea at Garur Chatti, and a visit to a small temple, where the courtyard floor was so hot to our bare feet that we had to skip about in agony, we trudged back to Muni-ki-Reti.

It was our last night sleeping beside the Ganga, and we rested with our chins in our hands, watching the river move silently past us, surging onward, India's lifeblood, inexorable and irresistible.

They say that if the Ganga ran dry, all life in India would cease. But, nourished by the eternal snows, it is the one river that can never run dry. As long as the mountains stand, the Ganga will flow to the sea, and millions will come to pay homage to its holy waters.

(1960)

# Mathura

Mathura, sacred above all cities, stands on the right bank of the Yamuna river, north-westward to the city of Agra. All men speak of it with reverence, for it is said, 'If a man spend in Benares all his lifetime, he has earned less merit than if he pass but a single day in the sacred city of Mathura.'

One cannot pierce the fog which hides the date of the city's birth, but holy it has always been, as the capital of Braj and the birthplace of Krishna who is the 'teacher and soul of the Universe, destroyer of the earth's tyrant kings and the First of the Spirits.'

We could not fail to be impressed by our journey to Mathura. All nature was alive and strange, and beautiful birds swept every now and then through the air to perch on the swinging telegraph wires: little birds with plumage the hue of emerald green; the long-tailed kingcrow; and innumerable doves in shades of blue and grey. And, resting on a telegraph pole, the great brown white-headed kite, which some say is Garuda, Vishnu's favourite steed. Resplendent too were the green and gold parrots, from among whom Kamadeva, the god of love, chose his steed. Armed with his sugar cane bow with its string made of bees, Kamadeva still rides at night over the plains of Mathura. Many and far are the journeys he makes on the nights approaching the full moon; he knows the way of men and women, and, like Cupid's, his bow is always ready to assist the ardent lover.

Legend tells us that Kamadeva, taking Spring as

his companion, started out one day to climb the mighty peaks of Himachal, and when they reached those snowy heights, the spring flowers bloomed around them although it was not the season of spring. Here they found great Siva; and the mischievous love-god, drawing his sugar cane bow, took aim at the mighty deity.

Siva, perhaps, would have pardoned the impudence with a great laugh, shaking all the world with its sound, but at that moment a lovely maiden, Parvati, the daughter of the mountain, came out to gather flowers to place as an oblation on his shrine, and anger consumed the great god. Siva's third and central eye gave forth a terrible stream of fire, and Kamadeva was burnt to ashes. This is what the holy books tell us, but when the westering sun finally lights up with its mellow radiance the temple walls of the holy city, Kamadeva is again ready to begin one of his nightly journeys on his resplendently plumaged parrot. Perhaps Parvati, the Maid of the Mountain, pleaded to the great one to restore the love-god, and Siva, forgetting his anger in her presence, gave back life to Kamadeva.

Journeying to Mathura, we could not fail to notice, in the tanks and jheels, an innumerable variety of game birds. All life is sacred for many miles around Mathura and not even the bird trapper is permitted to lay his snares. Every sheet of water is covered with a multitude of wild fowl, herons, cranes and many other waterbirds; while strutting underneath the shade of an aged tamarind tree are Krishna's sacred birds, the brilliant peacocks, who, long centuries ago, gave the city their name. Today Mathura is still called the Peacock City.

The peacocks know, in their regal pride, that they are the chosen of Krishna, and in twos and threes they may be seen spreading out their tails, brilliant-hued and fan-shaped, seen to perfection against a background of soft, rich verdure.

Here too, in the branches of the tamarind trees—and most of the trees of Mathura are tamarind—may be seen the light brown bottle-shaped nests of the weaver bird, lighted at night by the glow of the firefly, while on the surface of the water of marsh and lake floats a crimson waterweed.

Kamal and I sat in the shade of a thorn bush and watched a pair of Sarus cranes prancing and capering around each other: tall, stork-like birds, with naked red heads and long red legs.

'We might be Saruses in some future life,' I mused.

'That would be nice,' said Kamal. 'I wouldn't mind being a beautiful bird. I am not particular about being a man again, but I would not like to leave the world altogether.'

After a pause, he added: 'I'd like to be a sacred bird. I don't wish to be shot at.'

The Saruses were playing and making love. That appears to be their principal occupation apart from feeding on insects and small reptiles. The birds pair for life and are always very devoted companions. It is said that if one is killed its mate will haunt the scene for weeks, calling distractedly. They have even been known to pine away and die of grief. That is why they are held in such affection in the villages. Caught young, they can become delightful pets, and are as good as many watchdogs, emitting loud trumpet-like calls when disturbed.

'Many birds are sacred,' said Kamal, as a bluejay

swooped down from a tree and carried off a grass-hopper. Both the bluejay and Lord Siva are called Nilkanth. Siva has a blue throat, like the bird, because out of compassion for the human race he swallowed a deadly poison which was meant to destroy the world. He kept the poison in his throat and would not let it go any further.

'Are squirrels sacred?' asked Kamal, curiously watching one fumbling with a piece of bread which we had thrown away.

'Krishna loved squirrels. He would take them in his arms and stroke them with his long, gentle fingers. That is why they have four dark lines down their backs from head to tail. Krishna was very dark-skinned, and the lines are the marks of his fingers.'

'We should be gentle with animals,' said Kamal. 'We should not kill so many of them.'

I agreed with him: but while it is important that we do not kill them indiscriminately, it is also important that we respect them. We must acknowledge their rights on this earth. Everywhere, birds and animals are finding it more difficult to survive, because we are destroying their homes. They have to keep moving as the trees and the green grass and the forests disappear.

\* \* \*

In Mathura was born Krishna, the ancient, the pure and the immutable, who by his powers alone could annihilate the whole world. A mighty god was Krishna, and he lived in an abode upheld by the winds ten thousand millions of leagues above our world. But further and higher in the celestial paradise lived the beautiful Radha, his bride. But there arose a strife between her and Dharman, the demon spirit with lotus-red eyes, and Dharman cursed the beautiful maid, saying, 'Take thou a human form! Thou shall become a woman, to wander on the face of the earth.'

Radha appealed to Krishna, her lover, 'Dharman has cursed me, Lord. Tell me, O destroyer of fear, how can I endure life without you? You are my sight, my strength, and my highest riches.'

Krishna comforted Radha, saying, 'I too will go down to earth. Since you must be born there, descend with me. I will walk in the woodlands of Braj, waiting for you.'

Radha, riding on a boar, came to the face of the earth, and with her came Krishna, her Lord, the ruler of all the world. Krishna came to the city of Mathura in the kingdom of Braj, near the Yamuna river, and became the eighth son of Vasudeva and his beautiful wife, Princess Devaki, and his brother was the giant Balaram of many achievements.

There reigned at Mathura at that time the wicked tyrant Kamsa, the brother of Princess Devaki, who had thrust from the throne his father Ugrasen, and boastfully reigned in his place. No human monarch was he, but a mighty demon disguised in the form of a man. There was no safety then for priest or cattle, for he slew them all till the temple courts ran with blood.

Krishna grew up to manhood, and at length he slew the tyrant Kamsa and restored the throne to the aged Ugrasen.

\* \* \*

No one visits Mathura without also seeing Brindaban—the forest of Vrinda, who was once a mighty goddess. Brindaban, says the botanist, means a forest of tulsi trees.

Here, in this forest of Vrinda, lived Krishna and his brother Balaram as boys, and they ran wild in the woods, playing on their shepherds' pipes.

Brindaban lies north of Mathura on the same bank of the Yamuna. It stands on a tongue of land surrounded on three sides by the river, which has curved here in a strange fashion. Legend tells us that Balaram, the hero of great strength, once led a dance on the Yamuna's bank, but moved his giant limbs so clumsily that the river laughed aloud and taunted him: 'Forbear, O clumsy one! How can you hope to dance as Krishna, the youth divine?' Balaram was very angry with the river, and laying hold on his great plough, he traced a furrow, from the very brink of the stream, and so deep was the furrow, that the Yamuna fell into it, and Balaram led the river very far astray.

\* \* \*

A small temple marks the birthplace of Krishna, 'whose face is like the moon in an autumn festival', but more interesting are the remains of what are said to be the ruins of the palace of the tyrant Kamsa.

To this day visitors to the city of Mathura will be shown the mound where Kamsa's throne was set and the arena where his champions and his elephant were defeated by Krishna and Balaram.

We wandered in the streets of the city, past shops gleaming with the wealth of Mathura brasswork, while monkeys gambolled around seeking dainties. Passing through narrow streets, the river is at last reached. From the bridge one can see the riverface of Mathura with its innumerable temples. Below, on the banks of the sacred stream, are many bathers, and in the centre of the city's riverfront is the Vishram Ghat, 'the landing place of rest', where the two boy heroes rested after dragging the body of Kamsa down to the water's edge so that it might be laid on its funeral pyre. And near by is the watercourse, the ancient channel which the body of the demon king left in the riverside ground as he was dragged down to the water.

To see the majestic tortoises of Mathura we entered a boat and floated slowly down the river, gliding past bathing ghats and palaces and temples. We felt a thousand eyes were on us, and looking over the side saw the tortoises watching the boat and its occupants with grave interest. Often a bather would seize one of these long-necked creatures and hold it up to view. Immediately the tortoise would draw its legs into its shell, illustrating the Hindu tenet that nothing is annihilated but only disappears, the effect being absorbed in the cause.

(1960)

# Jaipur

As we still had a few days left of our holiday, and a little money, and as neither Kamal nor I was anxious to return to Delhi earlier than was necessary, we decided to sneak off to Jaipur for a day or two. We had both been to Jaipur before, but it is a city that one can visit again and again without ever tiring of its charm.

There is an atmosphere about Jaipur—once the most beautiful city in India, and one of the earliest planned cities in the world—which even to the casual visitor distinguishes it from other towns. This is probably due to the almost entire absence of any European or Western influence in the architecture and planning of the town.

Founded in 1728 by the brilliant astronomer-king Maharaja Jai Singh II, it is quite unlike any other town in India or Asia: no tortuous gloomy streets or squalid overcrowded bazaars. Its six main streets are very wide and straight, one running the whole length of the town, the others crossing it at right angles, dividing the city into rectangular blocks. These are enclosed by a high wall, its parapets loopholed for musketry, into which are set seven entrance gates.

On the north-west side the hills rise sheer beyond the city, bearing on their summit the Nahargarh or Tiger Fort. Not needed now for purposes of war, it houses much of the wealth of this former state's ruler. Guarded not by troops but by men of the robber caste, this wealth lay hoarded for centuries, potential but never used capital, typical of the ways of the East.

In the city itself, narrow streets are found in plenty, for a network of them connects the wide main roads. So narrow are some, that the bougainvillae sprawls from the upper storey of one building to its opposite across the way. But curiously enough, they are nearly all straight, and a passing glimpse from the main street reveals their whole length. Sometimes these lanes are full of little shops, but many of them contain only private houses, where occasionally a half-open door reveals a glimpse of the grass and fountain of a garden or courtyard beyond.

The great attraction of the main streets is their spaciousness and the beautiful facade of the tall buildings which line them, most colour-washed in a dull, pale old-rose tone, some showing the soft amber or grey of the original limestone. In some of them the plain walls are varied with beautiful little chhattris (umbrella-like structures), while here and there the old carved domes of some Jain temple break the flat line of roofs.

The street walls of these houses—which are really only the walls of the outer courtyard, the main building being behind and cut off from the street altogether—can boast of only the smallest windows, for these were meant to conceal, and not reveal, the zenana quarters behind. The quaint figures of elephants and other animals painted on the walls give them the appearance of dolls' houses when seen from the road below, though many of them are three or four storeys in height and from a distance look very imposing.

The streets themselves are a feast of colour and interest. Every mode of progression can be seen here, from ambling bullock-carts and *ekkas*, with their quaintly shaped and brightly coloured hoods, to buses and streamlined motor cars. There are strings of camels bearing fodder, and elephants that amble up the road to the Amber Palace, and here and there wanders the ubiquitous Brahmani bull. All along the streets and around the squares throng hundreds of pigeons— sacred birds throughout Rajasthan—being fed by the passers-by or helping themselves to food on the stalls.

All along the ground floor of the buildings, and cut off from them by a small projecting tin roof along which the langurs ran up and down in play, are the bazaar shops, little hives of industry doing a brisk trade. Busier still are the wide pavements in front; they are choc-a-bloc with stalls and with groups of artisans plying their trade in the midst of the passers-by.

We saw great piles of yellow maize and corn, of jawar and bajra, heaped upon the pavement, while to one side people were busy making the grain on primitive grindstones, laughing and singing as they ceaselessly wound the handle, three of them often working at one grinder. A little further on, what seemed at a distance to be a rich Herati rug flung down resolved itself into masses of chillies spread for yards along the pavement to dry in the sun. Then came the vegetables and fruit piled high in baskets, the countrywomen who had brought them squatting in the midst, sorting and selling and often nursing their babies at the same time.

Next came a little colony of brass workers sitting at the pavement's edge, engraving patterns on brass trays, plates and vessels, and then inlaying them with sticks of coloured enamel. Unlike them, the dyers generally work within their shops. In one of these we saw a whole family variously employed, from the old grandfather, who was mixing brilliant dyes in great brass cauldrons, to the latest infant, sitting in the middle and watching the others with an open mouth, while the family goat and attendant kid ambled in and out at will. Two of the family, a *pugree*-length of gaudy cloth just freshly dyed between them, walked up and down the pavement, waving it in the air to dry. The street had the appearance of being hung with bunting.

Most amusing of all, we came suddenly on three rows of little boys standing on the pavement with their slates at their feet. To one side stood the enterprising schoolmaster, while in front a small urchin with head craned forward loudly chanted the words of some lesson, which the class, in a medley of hoarse and squeaky voices, repeated after him. The intense concentration of this determined little group seemed in no way upset by the surrounding bustle and confusion.

There are few palaces in India to surpass the grandeur of the famous old palace of Amber. It lies north-west of the city, approached by a narrow pass in the hills which shuts off all view of Jaipur and opens on a little valley almost entirely closed by hills. Above a small lake, built on the barren hillside, stand the still perfect walls of this majestic fortress-palace. Their limestone blocks are mellowed to a soft amber colour, and the marble is now a rich cream.

The palace, now deserted except for its temple to the goddess Kali, is still in perfect condition. Its sun-soaked courtyards are open to the sky, and its empty pillared halls are full of echoes.

(1960)

# III

## Vignettes of Yesteryear

# Grandfather's Earthquake

'If ever there's a calamity,' Grandmother used to say, 'it will find Grandfather in his bath.' Grandfather loved his bath—which he took in a large round aluminium tub, and sometimes spent as long as an hour in it, 'wallowing', as he called it, and splashing around like a boy.

He was in his bath during the earthquake that convulsed Bengal and Assam on 12 June 1897—an earthquake so severe that even today the region of the great Brahmaputra river basin hasn't settled down. Not long ago it was reported that the entire Shillong plateau had moved an appreciable distance away from the Brahmaputra towards the Bay of Bengal. According to the Geological Survey of India, this shift has been taking place gradually over the past eighty years.

Had Grandfather been alive, he would have added one more clipping to his scrapbook on the earthquake. The clipping goes in anyway, because the scrapbook is now with the children. More than newspaper accounts of the disaster, it was Grandfather's own letters and memoirs that made the earthquake seem recent and vivid; for he, along with Grandmother and two of their children (one of them my father), was living in Shillong, a picturesque little hill station in Assam*, when the earth shook and the mountains heaved.

As I have mentioned, Grandfather was in his bath, splashing about, and did not hear the first rumbling. But Grandmother was in the garden, hanging out or

* This, of course, was a long time before the state of Meghalya, of which Shillong is now the capital, was created.

taking in the washing (she could never remember which) when, suddenly, the animals began making a hideous noise—a sure intimation of a natural disaster, for animals sense the approach of an earthquake much more quickly than humans.

The crows all took wing, wheeling wildly overhead and cawing loudly. The chickens flapped in circles, as if they were being chased. Two dogs sitting in the veranda suddenly jumped up and ran out with their tails between their legs. Within half a minute of her noticing the noise made by the animals, Grandmother heard a rattling, rumbling noise, like the approach of a train.

The noise increased for about a minute, and then there was the first trembling of the ground. The animals by this time all seemed to have gone mad. Treetops lashed backwards and forwards, doors banged and windows shook, and Grandmother swore later that the house actually swayed in front of her. She had difficulty in standing straight, though this could have been due more to the trembling of her knees than to the trembling of the ground.

The first shock lasted for about a minute and a half. 'I was in my tub having a bath,' Grandfather wrote for posterity, 'which for the first time in the last two months I had taken in the afternoon instead of in the morning. My wife and children and the ayah were downstairs. Then the shock came, accompanied by a loud rumbling sound under the earth and a quaking which increased in intensity every second. It was like putting so many shells in a basket and shaking them up with a rapid sifting motion from side to side.

'At first I did not realize what it was that caused my tub to sway about and the water to splash. I rose up, and found the earth heaving, while the wash-

80

stand, basin, sewer, cups and glasses danced and rocked about in the most hideous fashion. I rushed to the inner door to open it and search for wife and children, but could not move the dratted door as boxes, furniture and plaster had come up against it. The back door was the only way of escape. I managed to burst it open, and thank God, was able to get out. Sections of the thatched roof had slithered down on the four sides like a pack of cards and blocked all the exits and entrances.

'With only a towel wrapped around my waist, I ran out into the open to the front of the house, but found only my wife there. The whole front of the house was blocked by the fallen section of thatch from the roof. Through this I broke my way under the iron railings and extricated the others. The bearer had pluckily borne the weight of the whole thatched-roof section on his back as it had slithered down, and in this way saved the ayah and children from being crushed beneath it.'

After the main shock of the earthquake had passed, minor shocks took place at regular intervals of five minutes or so, all through the night. But during that first shake-up the town of Shillong was reduced to ruin and rubble. Everything made of masonry was brought to the ground. Government House, the post office, the jail, all tumbled down. When the jail fell, the prisoners, instead of making their escape, sat huddled on the road waiting for the superintendent to come to their aid.

'The ground began to heave and shake,' wrote a young girl in a newspaper called *The Englishman*\*. 'I

---

\* This later became *The Statesman*

stayed on my bicycle for a second, and then fell off and got up and tried to run, staggering about from side to side of the road. To my left I saw great clouds of dust, which I afterwards discovered to be houses falling and the earth slipping from the sides of the hills. To my right I saw the small dam at the end of the lake torn asunder and the water rushing out, the wooden bridge across the lake break in two and the sides of the lake falling in; and at my feet the ground cracking and opening. I was wild with fear and didn't know which way to turn.'

The lake rose up like a mountain, and then totally disappeared, leaving only a swamp of red mud. Not a house was left standing. People were rushing about, wives looking for husbands, parents looking for children, not knowing whether their loved ones were alive or dead. A crowd of people had collected on the cricket ground, which was considered the safest place; but Grandfather and the family took shelter in a small shop on the road outside his house. The shop was a rickety wooden structure, which had always looked as though it would fall down in a strong wind. But it withstood the earthquake.

And then the rain came and it poured. This was extraordinary, because before the earthquake there wasn't a cloud to be seen; but, five minutes after the shock, Shillong was enveloped in cloud and mist. The shock was felt for more than a hundred miles on the Assam-Bengal Railway. A train was overturned at Shamshernagar; another was derailed at Mantolla. Over a thousand people lost their lives in the Cherrapunji Hills, and in other areas, too, the death toll was heavy.

The Brahmaputra burst its banks and many

cultivators were drowned in the flood. A tiger was found drowned. And in North Bhagalpur, where the earthquake started, two elephants sat down in the bazaar and refused to get up until the following morning.

Over a hundred men who were at work in Shillong's government printing press were caught in the building when it collapsed, and though the men of a Gurkha regiment did splendid rescue work only a few were brought out alive. One of those killed in Shillong was Mr McCabe, a British official. Grandfather described the ruins of Mr McCabe's house: 'Here a bedpost, there a sword, a broken desk or chair, a bit of torn carpet, a well-known hat with its Indian Civil Service colours, battered books, all speaking reminiscences of the man we mourn.'

While most houses collapsed where they stood, Government House, it seems, 'fell backwards'. The church was a mass of red stones in ugly disorder. The organ was a tortured wreck.

A few days later the family, with other refugees, were making their way to Calcutta to stay with friends or relatives. It was a slow, tedious journey, with many interruptions, for the roads and railway lines had been badly damaged and passengers had often to be transported in trolleys. Grandfather was rather struck at the stoicism displayed by an assistant engineer. At one station a telegram was handed to the engineer informing him that his bungalow had been destroyed. 'Beastly nuisance,' he observed with an aggrieved air. 'I've seen it cave in during a storm, but this is the first time it has played me such a trick on account of an earthquake.'

The family got to Calcutta to find the inhabitants of the capital in a panic; for they too had felt the quake and were expecting it to recur. The damage in Calcutta was slight compared to the devastation elsewhere, but nerves were on edge, and people slept in the open or in carriages. Cracks and fissures had appeared in a number of old buildings, and Grandfather was among the many who were worried at the proposal to fire a salute of sixty guns on Jubilee Day (the Diamond Jubilee of Queen Victoria); they felt the gunfire would bring down a number of shaky buildings. Obviously Grandfather did not wish to be caught in his bath a second time. However, Queen Victoria was not to be deprived of her salute. The guns were duly fired, and Calcutta remained standing.

# Kipling's Simla

Every March, when the rhododendrons stain the slopes crimson with their blooms, a sturdy little steam engine goes huffing and puffing through the 103 tunnels between Kalka and Simla.

This is probably the most picturesque and romantic way of approaching the hill station, although the journey by road is much quicker. But quite recently I went to Simla by a little-used route, the road from Dehra Dun via Nahan and Solan. It takes one first through the sub-tropical Siwaliks, and then after Nahan into the foothills and some beautiful and extensive pine forests, before joining the main highway near Solan. By bus it is a tedious ten-hour journey, but by car it is a picturesque ride, and there is very little traffic to contend with. . .

But those train journeys stand out in memory—the little restaurant at Barog, just before the train reaches Dharampur, where the roads for Sanawar and Kasauli branch off; and the gorge at Tara Devi, opening out to give the weary traveller the splendid and uplifting panorama of the city of Simla straddling the side of the mountain.

In Rudyard Kipling's time (that is, in the 1870s and '80s), travellers spent the night at Kalka and then covered the sixty-odd hill miles by tonga, a rugged and exhausting journey. It was especially hard on invalids who had travelled long distances to recuperate in the cool clear air of the mountains.

In his story 'The Other Man' (*Plain Tales from the*

*Hills; 1890)*, Kipling describes the unhappy results of the tonga-ride on one such visitor:

'Sitting on the back seat, very square and firm, with one hand on the awning stanchion and the wet pouring off his hat and moustache, was the Other Man—dead. The sixty-mile uphill jolt had been too much for his valve, I suppose. The tonga driver said, "This Sahib died two stages out of Solan. Therefore, I tied him with a rope, lest he should fall out by the way, and so we came to Simla. Will the Sahib give me *bakshish*?" It, pointing to the Other Man, "should have given one rupee."'

Today's visitor to Simla need have no qualms about the journey by road, which is swift and painless (provided you drive carefully), but the coolies at the Simla bus stand will be found to be as adamant as Kipling's tonga-driver in claiming their *bakshish*.

Simla is worth a visit at any time of the year, even during the monsoon. The monsoon season is one of the most beautiful times of the year in the Himalayas, with the mist trailing up the valleys, and the hill slopes a lush green, thick with ferns and wild flowers. The call of the kastura, or whistling-thrush, can be heard in every glen, while the barbet cries insistently from the treetops.

Not far from Christ Church is the corner where a great fictional character, Lurgan Sahib, had his shop—Lurgan being the curio-dealer who took the young Kim in hand and trained him as a spy. He was based on a real-life character, who had his shop here. Kipling wrote *Kim* a few years after he had left India. His nostalgia for India, and in particular for the hills, come through in his description of Kim's arrival in Simla in the company of the Afghan horse-dealer, Mahbub Ali.

' "A fair land—a most beautiful land is this of Hind—and the land of the Five Rivers is fairer than all," Kim half-chanted. "Into it I will go again. . . Once gone, who shall find me? Look, Hajji, is yonder the city of Simla? Allah! What a city!" '

They led their horses below the main road into the lower Simla bazaar—'the crowded rabbit-warren that climbs up from the valley to the Town Hall at an angle of forty-five!' And then together they set off 'through the mysterious dusk, full of the noises of a city below the hillside and the breath of a cool wind in deodar-crowned Jakko, shouldering the stars.'

Shouldering the stars! That is how I always think of Simla—standing on the Ridge and looking up through the clear air into the vault of the heavens, where the stars seem so much nearer. . . And they are reflected below, in the myriad lights of the shops and houses.

\* \* \*

For those who want a bit of history, Simla came into being at the end of the Anglo-Gurkha War (1814-16), when most of the surrounding district—captured by the Gurkhas during their invasion—was restored to various states; but the land on which Simla stands was retained by the British—'for services rendered'! Lieutenant Rose built the first house, a thatched wooden cottage, in 1819. His successor, Lieutenant Kennedy, in 1822 built a permanent house, which survived until it was destroyed in a fire a couple of years ago. In 1827 Lord Amherst spent several months at Kennedy House and from then on Simla grew in favour with the British. Its early history can be read in more detail in Sir Edward Buck's *Simla Past and*

*Present,* copies of which sometimes turn up in second-hand bookshops.

From 1865 until the Second World War, Simla was the summer capital of the Government of India. Later it served as the capital of East Punjab pending the construction of Chandigarh, and today of course it is the capital of Himachal Pradesh.

It is not, however, as a capital city that Simla attracts the visitor but as a place of lovely winding walks, magnificent views, and romantic links with the past. Compared with some of our other hill stations, it is well looked after; the streets are clean and uncluttered, the old Georgian-style buildings still stand. And the trees are more in evidence than at other hill resorts.

Simla has a special place in my affections. It was there that I went to school, and it was there that my father and I spent our happiest times together.

We stayed on Elysium Hill; took long walks to Kasumpti and around Jakko Hill; sipped milk-shakes at Davico's; saw plays at the Gaiety Theatre (happily still in existence); fed the monkeys at the temple on Jakko; picnicked in Chhota Simla. All this during the short summer break when my father (on leave from the Air Force) came up to see me. He told me stories of phantom-rickshaws and enchanted forests and planted in me the seeds of my writing career. I was only ten when he died. But he had already passed on to me his love for the hills. And even after I had finished school and grown to manhood, I was to return to the hills again and again—to Simla and Mussoorie, Himachal and Garhwal—because once the mountains are in your blood, there is no escape.

\* \* \*

Simla beckons. I must return. And, like Kim, I will take the last bend near Summer Hill and look up and exclaim: 'Ah! What a city!'

'Romance brought up the nine-fifteen,' wrote Kipling and there is still romance to be found on trains and at lonely stations. Small wayside stations have always fascinated me. Manned sometimes by just one or two men, and often situated in the middle of a damp sub-tropical forest, or clinging to the mountain side on the way to Simla or Darjeeling, these little stations are, for me, outposts of romance, lonely symbols of the spirit that led a certain kind of pioneer to lay tracks into the remote corners of the earth.

Recently I was at such a wayside stop, on a line that went through the Terai forests near the foothills of the Himalayas. At about ten at night, the *khilasi*, or station watchman, lit his kerosene lamp and started walking up the track into the jungle. He was a Gujar, and his true vocation was the keeping of buffaloes, but the breaking up of his tribe had led him into this strange new occupation.

'Where are you going?' I asked.

'To see if the tunnel is clear,' he said. 'The Mail train comes in twenty minutes.'

So I went with him, a furlong or two along the tracks, through a deep cutting which led to the tunnel. Every night, the *khilasi* walked though the dark tunnel, and then stood outside to wave his lamp to the oncoming train as a signal that the track was clear. If the engine driver did not see the lamp, he stopped the train. It always slowed down near the cutting. Having inspected the tunnel, we stood outside, waiting for the train. It seemed a long time coming. There was no moon, and the dense forest seemed to be trying to crowd us into the narrow cutting. The sounds of the forest came to us on the night wind—the belling of a sambar, the cry of a fox, told us that perhaps a tiger or a leopard was on the prowl. There were strange nocturnal bird and insect sounds; and then silence.

The *khilasi* stood outside the tunnel, trimming his lamp, listening to the faint sounds of the jungle—sounds which only he, a Gujar who had grown up on the fringe of the forest, could identify and understand. Something made him stand very still for a few moments, peering into the darkness, and I could sense that everything was not as it should be.

'There is something in the tunnel,' he said.

I could hear nothing at first; but then there came a regular sawing sound, just like the sound of someone sawing through the branch of a tree.

'*Baghera*!' whispered the *khilasi*. He had said enough to enable me to recognize the sound—that of a leopard trying to find its mate.

I thought how fortunate we were that it had not been there when we walked through the tunnel. A leopard is unpredictable. But so is a *khilasi*.

'The train will be coming soon,' he whispered urgently, 'we must drive the animal out of the tunnel, or it will be killed.'

He must have sensed my astonishment, because he said, 'Do not worry, sahib. I know this leopard well. We have seen each other many times. He has a weakness for stray dogs and goats, but he will not harm us.'

He gave me his small hand-axe to hold, and, raising his lamp high, started walking into the tunnel, shouting at the top of his voice to try and scare away the animal. I followed close behind him.

We had gone about twenty yards into the tunnel when the light from the *khilasi's* lamp fell on the leopard, who was crouching between the tracks, only about fifteen feet from us.

He was not a big leopard, but he was lithe and sinewy. Baring his teeth in a snarl, he went down on his belly, tail twitching, and I felt sure he was going to spring.

The *khilasi* and I both shouted together. Our voices rang and echoed through the tunnel. And the frightened leopard, uncertain of how many human beings were in there with him, turned swiftly and disappeared into the darkness.

As we returned to the tunnel entrance, the rails began to hum and we knew the train was coming.

I put my hand to one of the rails and felt its tremor. And then the engine came round the bend, hissing at us, scattering sparks into the darkness, defying the jungle as it roared through the steep sides of the cutting. It charged straight at the tunnel, and into it, thundering past us like some beautiful dragon from my childhood dreams. And when it had gone the silence returned, and the forest breathed again. Only the rails still trembled with the passing of the train.

As they tremble now to the passing of my own train, rushing through the night with its complement of precious humans, while somewhere at a lonely cutting in the foothills, a small thin man, who must always remain a firefly to these travelling thousands, lights up the darkness for steam engines and panthers.

And yet, for the *khilasi* himself, the incident I have recalled was not an adventure; it was a duty, a job of work, an everyday incident.

For me, all are significant: the lighted compartment with its farmers, shopkeepers, artisans, clerks and occasional pickpockets; and the lonely wayside stop, with its uncorrupted lamplighter.

Romance still rides the nine-fifteen.

# Life with Uncle Ken

## Granny's Fabulous Kitchen

As kitchens went, it wasn't all that big. It wasn't as big as the bedroom or the living room, but it was big enough, and there was a pantry next to it. What made it fabulous was all that came out of it: good things to eat like cakes and curries, chocolate fudge and peanut toffee, jellies and jam tarts, meat pies, stuffed turkeys, stuffed chickens, stuffed eggplants, and hams stuffed with stuffed chickens.

As far as I was concerned, Granny was the best cook in the whole wide world.

Two generations of Clerkes had lived in India and my maternal grandmother had settled in a small town in the foothills, just where the great plain ended and the Himalayas began. The town was called Dehra Dun. It's still there, though much bigger and busier now. Granny had a house, a large rambling bungalow, on the outskirts of the town, on Old Survey Road. In the grounds were many trees, most of them fruit trees. Mangoes, lichees, guavas, bananas, papayas, lemons—there was room for all of them, including a giant jackfruit tree casting its shadow on the walls of the house.

> Blessed is the house upon whose walls
> The shade of an old tree softly falls. . .

I remember those lines of Granny's. They were true words, because it was a good house to live in, especially for a nine-year-old with a tremendous appetite. If Granny was the best cook in the world, I must have been the boy with the best appetite.

Every winter, when I came home from boarding school, I would spend about a month with Granny before going on to spend the rest of the holidays with my mother and stepfather. My parents couldn't cook. They employed a *khansama*—a professional cook—who made a good mutton curry but little else. Mutton curry for lunch and mutton curry for dinner can be a bit tiring, especially for a boy who liked to eat almost everything.

Granny was glad to have me because she lived alone most of the time. Not entirely alone, though. . . There was a gardener, Dhuki, who lived in an outhouse. And he had a son called Mohan, who was about my age. And there was Ayah, an elderly maidservant, who helped with the household work. And there was a Siamese cat with bright blue eyes, and a mongrel dog called Crazy because he ran circles round the house.

And of course there was Uncle Ken, Granny's nephew, who came to stay whenever he was out of a job (which was quite often) or when he felt like enjoying some of Granny's cooking.

So Granny wasn't really alone. All the same, she was glad to have me. She didn't enjoy cooking for herself, she said; she had to cook for *someone*. And although the cat and the dog and sometimes Uncle Ken appreciated her efforts, a good cook likes to have a boy to feed, because boys are adventurous and ready to try the most unusual dishes.

Whenever Granny tried out a new recipe on me, she would wait for my comments and reactions, and then make a note in one of her exercise books. These notes were useful when she made the dish again, or when she tried it out on others.

'Do you like it?' she'd ask, after I'd taken a few mouthfuls.

'Yes, Gran.'

'Sweet enough?'

'Yes, Gran.'

'Not *too* sweet?'

'No, Gran.'

'Would you like some more?'

'Yes, please, Gran.'

'Well, finish it off.'

'If you say so, Gran.'

\* \* \*

Roast Duck. This was one of Granny's specials. The first time I had roast duck at Granny's place, Uncle Ken was there too.

He'd just lost a job as a railway guard, and had come to stay with Granny until he could find another job. He always stayed as long as he could, only moving on when Granny offered to get him a job as an assistant master in Padre Lal's Academy for Small Boys. Uncle Ken couldn't stand small boys. They made him nervous, he said. I made him nervous too, but there was only one of me, and there was always Granny to protect him. At Padre Lal's, there were over a hundred small boys.

Although Uncle Ken had a tremendous appetite, and ate just as much as I did, he never praised Granny's dishes. I think this is why I was annoyed with him at times, and why sometimes I enjoyed making him feel nervous.

Uncle Ken looked down at the roast duck, his glasses slipping down to the edge of his nose.

'Hm . . . Duck again, Aunt Ellen?'

'What do you mean, duck again? You haven't had duck since you were here last month.'

'That's what I mean,' said Uncle Ken. 'Somehow, one expects more variety from you, Aunt.'

All the same, he took two large helpings and ate most of the stuffing before I could get at it. I took my revenge by emptying all the apple sauce onto my plate. Uncle Ken knew I loved the stuffing; and I knew he was crazy about Granny's apple sauce. So we were even.

'When are you joining your parents?' he asked hopefully, over the jam tart.

'I may not go to them this year,' I said. 'When are you getting another job, Uncle?'

'Oh, I'm thinking of taking a rest for a couple of months.'

I enjoyed helping Granny and Ayah with the washing up. While we were at work, Uncle Ken would take a siesta on the veranda or switch on the radio to listen to dance music. Glenn Miller and his Swing Band was all the rage then.

'And how do you like your Uncle Ken?' asked Granny one day, as she emptied the bones from his plate into the dog's bowl.

'I wish he was someone else's Uncle,' I said.

'He's not so bad, really. Just eccentric.'

'What's eccentric?'

'Oh, just a little crazy.'

'At least Crazy runs round the house,' I said. 'I've never seen Uncle Ken running.'

\* \* \*

But I did one day.

Mohan and I were playing marbles in the shade of the mango grove when we were taken aback by the sight of Uncle Ken charging across the compound, pursued by a swarm of bees. He'd been smoking a cigar under a silk-cotton tree, and the fumes had disturbed the wild bees in their hive, directly above him. Uncle Ken fled indoors and leapt into a tub of cold water. He had received a few stings and decided to remain in bed for three days. Ayah took his meals to him on a tray.

'I didn't know Uncle Ken could run so fast,' I said, later that day.

'It's nature's way of compensating,' said Granny.

'What's compensating?'

'Making up for things. . . Now at least Uncle Ken knows that he can run. Isn't that wonderful?'

\* \* \*

Whenever Granny made vanilla or chocolate fudge, she gave me some to take to Mohan, the gardener's son. It was no use taking him roast duck or curried chicken, because in his house no one ate meat. But Mohan liked sweets—Indian sweets, which were made with lots of milk and lots of sugar, as well as Granny's home-made English sweets.

We would climb into the branches of the jackfruit tree and eat fudge or peppermints or sticky toffee.

We couldn't eat the jackfruit, except when it was cooked as a vegetable or made into a pickle. But the tree itself was wonderful for climbing. And some wonderful creatures lived in it—squirrels and fruit-bats and a pair of green parrots. The squirrels were friendly and soon got into the habit of eating from our hands. They, too, were fond of chocolate fudge. One young squirrel would even explore my pockets to see if I was keeping anything from him.

Mohan and I could climb almost any tree in the garden, and if Granny was looking for us, she'd call from the front veranda and then from the back veranda and then from the pantry at the side of the house and finally from her bathroom window on the other side of the house. There were trees on all sides, and it was impossible to tell which one we were in, until we answered her call. Sometimes Crazy would give us away by barking beneath our tree.

When there was fruit to be picked, Mohan did the picking. The mangoes and lichees came into season during the summer, when I was away at boarding school, so I couldn't help with the fruit gathering. The papayas were in season during the winter, but you don't climb papaya trees, they are too slender and wobbly. You knock the papayas down with a long pole.

Mohan also helped Granny with the pickling. She was justly famous for her pickles. Green mangoes, pickled in oil, were always popular. So was her hot lime pickle. And she was equally good at pickling turnips, carrots, cauliflowers, chillies, and other fruits and vegetables. She could pickle almost anything, from a nasturtium seed to a jackfruit Uncle Ken didn't care for pickles, so I was always urging Granny to make more of them.

My own preference was for sweet chutneys and sauces, but I ate pickles too, even the very hot ones.

One winter, when Granny's funds were low, Mohan and I went from house to house, selling pickles for her.

Inspite of all the people and pets she fed, Granny wasn't rich. The house had come to her from Grandfather, but there wasn't much money in the bank. The mango crop brought in a fair amount every year, and there was a small pension from the Railways (Grandfather had been one of the pioneers who'd helped bring the railway line to Dehra at the turn of the century), but there was no other income. And now that I come to think of it, all those wonderful meals consisted only of the one course, followed by a sweet dish. It was Granny's cooking that turned a modest meal into a feast.

I wasn't ashamed to sell pickles for Granny. It was great fun. Mohan and I armed ourselves with baskets filled with pickle bottles, then set off to cover all the houses in our area.

Major Wilkie, across the road, was our first customer. He had a red beard and bright blue eyes and was almost always good-humoured.

'And what have you got there, young Bond?' he asked

'Pickles, sir.'

'Pickles! Have you been making them?'

'No, sir, they're my grandmother's. We're selling them, so we can buy a turkey for Christmas.'

'Mrs Clerke's pickles, eh? Well, I'm glad mine is the first house on your way, because I'm sure that basket will soon be empty. There is no one who can make a pickle like your grandmother, son, I've said it before and I'll say it again, she's God's gift to a world that's terribly short of good cooks. My wife's gone shopping, so I can talk quite freely, you see . . . What have you got this time? Stuffed chillies, I trust. She knows they're my favourite. I shall be deeply wounded if there are no stuffed chillies in that basket.'

There were, in fact, three bottles of stuffed red chillies in the basket, and Major Wilkie took all of them.

Our next call was at Miss Kellner's house. Miss Kellner couldn't eat hot food, so it was no use offering her pickles. But she bought a bottle of preserved ginger. And she gave me a little prayer book. Whenever I went to see her, she gave me a new prayer book. Soon I had quite a collection of prayer books. What was I to do with them? Finally, Uncle Ken took them off me, and sold them to the Children's Academy.

Further down the road, Dr Dutt, who was in charge of the hospital, bought several bottles of lime pickles, saying it was good for his liver. And Mr Hari, who owned a garage at the end of the road and sold all the latest cars, bought two bottles of pickled onions and begged us to bring him another two the following month.

By the time we got home, the basket would usually be empty, and Granny richer by twenty or thirty rupees—enough, in those days, for a turkey.

\* \* \*

'It's high time you found a job,' said Granny to Uncle Ken one day.

'There are no jobs in Dehra,' complained Uncle Ken.

'How can you tell? You've never looked for one. And anyway, you don't have to stay here for ever. Your sister Emily is headmistress of a school in Lucknow. You could go to her. She said before that she was ready to put you in charge of a dormitory.'

'Bah! said Uncle Ken. 'Honestly, Aunt, you don't expect me to look after a dormitory seething with forty or fifty demented small boys?'

'What's demented?' I asked.

'Shut up,' said Uncle Ken.

'It means crazy,' said Granny.

'So many words mean crazy,' I complained. 'Why don't we just say crazy. We have a crazy dog, and now Uncle Ken is crazy too.'

Uncle Ken clipped me over my ear, and Granny said, 'Your Uncle isn't crazy, so don't be disrespectful. He's just lazy.'

'And eccentric,' I said. 'I heard he was eccentric.'

'Who said I was eccentric?' demanded Uncle Ken.

'Miss Leslie,' I lied. I knew Uncle Ken was fond of Miss Leslie, who ran a beauty parlour in Dehra's smart shopping centre, Astley Hall.

'I don't believe you,' said Uncle Ken. 'Anyway, when did you see Miss Leslie?'

'We sold her a bottle of mint chutney last week. I told her you liked mint chutney. But she said she'd bought it for Mr Brown who's taking her to the pictures tomorrow.'

\* \* \*

'Eat well, but don't overeat,' Granny used to tell me. 'Good food is a gift from God, and like any other gift, it can be misused.'

She'd made a list of kitchen proverbs and pinned it to the pantry door—not so high that I couldn't read it, either.

These were some of the proverbs:

LIGHT SUPPERS MAKE LONG LIVES.
BETTER A SMALL FISH THAN AN EMPTY DISH.
THERE IS SKILL IN ALL THINGS, EVEN IN
    MAKING PORRIDGE.
EATING AND DRINKING SHOULD NOT KEEP
    MEN FROM THINKING.
DRY BREAD AT HOME IS BETTER THAN
    ROAST MEAT ABROAD.
A GOOD DINNER SHARPENS THE WIT AND
    SOFTENS THE HEART.
LET NOT YOUR TONGUE CUT YOUR THROAT.

**Uncle Ken Does Nothing**

To our surprise, Uncle Ken got a part-time job as a guide, showing tourists the 'sights' around Dehra.

There was an old fort near the riverbed; and a seventeenth-century temple; and a jail where Pandit Nehru had spent some time as a political prisoner; and, about ten miles into the foothills, the hot sulphur springs.

Uncle Ken told us he was taking a party of six American tourists, husbands and wives, to the sulphur springs. Granny was pleased. Uncle Ken was busy at last! She gave him a hamper filled with ham sandwiches, home-made biscuits and a dozen oranges —ample provision for a day's outing.

The sulphur springs were only ten miles from Dehra, but we didn't see Uncle Ken for three days.

He was a sight when he got back. His clothes were dusty and torn; his cheeks were sunken; and the little bald patch on top of his head had been burnt a bright red.

'What have you been doing to yourself?' asked Granny.

Uncle Ken sank into the armchair on the veranda. 'I'm starving, Aunt Ellen. Give me something to eat.'

'What happened to the food you took with you?'

'There were seven of us, and it was all finished on the first day.'

'Well it was only supposed to last a day. You said you were going to the sulphur springs.'

'Yes, that's where we were going,' said Uncle Ken. 'But we never reached them. We got lost in the hills.'

'How could you possibly have got lost in the hills? You had only to walk straight along the riverbed and up the valley . . . *You* ought to know, you were the guide and you'd been there before, when my husband was alive.'

'Yes, I know,' said Uncle Ken, looking crestfallen. 'But I forgot the way. That is, I forgot the valley. I mean, I took them up the wrong valley. And I kept thinking the springs would be at the same river, but it wasn't the same river . . . So we kept walking, until we were in the hills, and then I looked down and saw we'd come up the wrong valley. We had to spend the night under the stars. It was very, very cold. And next day I thought we'd come back a quicker way, through Mussoorie, but we took the wrong path and reached Kempti instead . . . And then we walked down to the motor-road and caught a bus.'

I helped Granny put Uncle Ken to bed, and then I

helped her make him a strengthening onion soup. I took him the soup on a tray, and he made a face while drinking it and then asked for more. He was in bed for two days, while Ayah and I took turns taking him his meals. He wasn't a bit graceful.

\* \* \*

When Uncle Ken complained he was losing his hair and that his bald patch was increasing in size, Granny looked up her book of old recipes and said there was one for baldness which Grandfather had used with great success. It consisted of a lotion made with gherkins soaked in brandy. Uncle Ken said he'd try it.

Granny soaked some gherkins in brandy for a week, then gave the bottle to Uncle Ken with instructions to rub a little into his scalp mornings and evenings.

Next day, when she looked into his room, she found only gherkins in the bottle. Uncle Ken had drunk all the brandy.

\* \* \*

Uncle Ken liked to whistle.

Hands in his pockets, nothing to do, he would stroll about the house, around the garden, up and down the road, whistling feebly to himself.

It was always the same whistle, tuneless to everyone except my uncle.

'What are you whistling today, Uncle Ken?' I'd ask.

'"Ol' Man River". Don't you recognize it?'

And the next time around he'd be whistling the

same notes, and I'd say, 'Still whistling "Ol' Man River", Uncle?'

'No, I'm not. This is "Danny Boy". Can't you tell the difference?'

And he'd slouch off, whistling tunelessly.

Sometimes it irritated Granny.

'Can't you stop whistling, Ken? It gets on my nerves. Why don't you try singing for a change?'

'I can't. It's "The Blue Danube", there aren't any words,' and he'd waltz around the kitchen, whistling.

'Well, you can do your whistling and waltzing on the veranda,' Granny would say. 'I won't have it in the kitchen. It spoils the food.'

When Uncle Ken had a bad tooth removed by our dentist, Dr Kapadia, we thought his whistling would stop. But it only became louder and shriller.

One day, while he was strolling along the road, hands in his pockets, doing nothing, whistling very loudly, a girl on a bicycle passed him. She stopped suddenly, got off the bicycle, and blocked his way.

'If you whistle at me every time I pass, Kenneth Clerke,' she said, 'I'll wallop you!'

Uncle Ken went red in the face. 'I wasn't whistling at you,' he said.

'Well, I don't see anyone else on the road.'

'I was whistling "God Save The King". Don't you recognize it?'

## Uncle Ken on the job

'We'll have to do something about Uncle Ken,' said Granny to the world at large.

I was in the kitchen with her, shelling peas and popping a few into my mouth now and then. Suzie, the Siamese cat, sat on the sideboard, patiently watching Granny prepare an Irish stew. Suzie liked Irish stew.

'It's not that I mind him staying,' said Granny, 'and I don't want any money from him, either. But it isn't healthy for a young man to remain idle for so long.'

'Is Uncle Ken a young man, Gran?'

'He's forty. Everyone says he'll improve as he grows up.'

'He could go and live with Aunt Mabel.'

'He *does* go and live with Aunt Mabel. He also lives with Aunt Emily and Aunt Beryl. That's his trouble—he has too many doting sisters ready to put him up and put up with him. . . Their husbands are all quite well-off and can afford to have him now and then. So our Ken spends three months with Mabel, three months with Beryl, three months with me. That way he gets through the year as everyone's guest and doesn't have to worry about making a living.'

'He's lucky in a way,' I said.

'His luck won't last for ever. Already Mabel is talking of going to New Zealand. And once India is free—in just a year or two from now—Emily and Beryl will probably go off to England, because their husbands are in the Army and all the British officers will be leaving.'

'Can't Uncle Ken follow them to England?'

'He knows he'll have to start working if he goes there. When your aunts find they have to manage without servants, they won't he ready to keep Ken for long periods. In any case, who's going to pay his fare to England or New Zealand?'

'If he can't go, he'll stay here with you, Granny. You'll be here, won't you?'

'Not for ever. Only while I live.'

'You won't go to England?'

'No, I've grown up here. I'm like the trees. I've taken root, I won't be going away—not until, like an old tree, I'm without any more leaves . . . You'll go, though, when you are bigger. You'll probably finish your schooling abroad.'

'I'd rather finish it here. I want to spend all my holidays with you. If I go away, who'll look after you when you grow old?'

'I'm old already. Over sixty.'

'Is that very old? It's only a little older than Uncle Ken. And how will you look after him when you're *really* old?'

'He can look after himself if he tries. And it's time he started. It's time he took a job.'

I pondered on the problem. I could think of nothing that would suit Uncle Ken—or rather, I could think of no one who would find him suitable. It was Ayah who made a suggestion.

'The Maharani of Jetpur needs a tutor for her children,' she said. 'Just a boy and a girl.'

'How do you know?' asked Granny.

'I heard it from their ayah. The pay is two hundred rupees a month, and there is not much work—only two hours every morning.'

'That should suit Uncle Ken,' I said.

'Yes, it's a good idea,' said Granny. 'We'll have to talk him into applying. He ought to go over and see them. The Maharani is a good person to work for.'

Uncle Ken agreed to go over and enquire about

107

the job. The Maharani was out when he called, but he was interviewed by the Maharaja.

'Do you play tennis?' asked the Maharaja.

'Yes,' said Uncle Ken, who remembered having played a bit of tennis when he was a schoolboy.

'In that case, the job's yours. I've been looking for a fourth player for a doubles match . . . By the way, were you at Cambridge?'

'No, I was at Oxford,' said Uncle Ken.

The Maharaja was impressed. An Oxford man who could play tennis was just the sort of tutor he wanted for his children.

When Uncle Ken told Granny about the interview, she said, 'But you haven't been to Oxford, Ken. How could you say that!'

'Of course I have been to Oxford. Don't you remember? I spent two years there with your brother Jim!'

'Yes, but you were helping him in his pub in the town. You weren't at the University.'

'Well, the Maharaja never asked me if I had been to the University. He asked me if I was at Cambridge, and I said no, I was at Oxford, which was perfectly true. He didn't ask me what I was doing at Oxford. What difference does it make?' And he strolled off, whistling.

\* \* \*

To our surprise, Uncle Ken was a great success in his job. In the beginning, anyway.

The Maharaja was such a poor tennis player that he was delighted to discover that there was someone who was even worse. So, instead of becoming a doubles partner for the Maharaja, Uncle Ken became his favourite singles opponent. As long as he could keep losing to His Highness, Uncle Ken's job was safe.

In between tennis matches and accompanying his employer on duck shoots, Uncle Ken squeezed in a few lessons for the children, teaching them reading, writing and arithmetic. Sometimes he took me along, so that I could tell him when he got his sums wrong. Uncle Ken wasn't very good at subtraction, although he could add fairly well.

The Maharaja's children were smaller than me. Uncle Ken would leave me with them, saying, 'Just see that they do their sums properly, Ruskin,' and he would stroll off to the tennis courts, hands in his pockets, whistling tunelessly.

Even if his pupils had different answers to the same sum, he would give both of them an encouraging pat, saying, 'Excellent, excellent. I'm glad to see both of you trying so hard. One of you is right and one of you is wrong, but as I don't want to discourage either of you, I won't say who's right and who's wrong!'

But afterwards, on the way home, he'd ask me: 'Which was the right answer, Ruskin?'

\* \* \*

Uncle Ken always maintained that he would never have lost his job if he hadn't beaten the Maharaja at tennis.

Not that Uncle Ken had any intention of winning. But by playing occasional games with the Maharaja's secretaries and guests, his tennis had improved and so, try as hard as he might to lose, he couldn't help winning a match against his employer.

The Maharaja was furious.

'Mr Clerke,' he said sternly, 'I don't think you realize the importance of losing. We can't all win, you know. Where would the world be without losers?'

'I'm terribly sorry,' said Uncle Ken. 'It was just a fluke, your Highness.'

The Maharaja accepted Uncle Ken's apologies; but a week later it happened again. Keneth Clerke won and the Maharaja stormed off the court without saying a word. The following day he turned up at lesson time. As usual Uncle Ken and the children were engaged in a game of noughts and crosses.

'We won't be requiring your services from tomorrow, Mr Clerke. I've asked my secretary to give you a month's salary in lieu of notice.'

Uncle Ken came home with his hands in his pockets, whistling cheerfully.

'You're early,' said Granny.

'They don't need me any more,' said Uncle Ken.

'Oh well, never mind. Come in and have your tea.'

Granny must have known the job wouldn't last very long. And she wasn't one to nag. As she said later, 'At least he tried. And it lasted longer than most of his jobs—two months.'

## Uncle Ken at the Wheel

On my next visit to Dehra, Mohan met me at the station. We got into a tonga with my luggage and we went rattling and jingling along Dehra's quiet roads to Granny's hose.

'Tell me all the news, Mohan.'

'Not much to tell. Some of the sahibs are selling their houses and going away. Suzie has had kittens.'

Granny knew I'd been in the train for two nights, and she had a huge breakfast ready for me. Porridge, scrambled eggs on toast. Bacon with fried tomatoes. Toast and marmalade. Sweet milky tea.

She told me there'd been a letter from Uncle Ken.

'He says he's the assistant manager in Firpo's hotel in Simla,' she said. 'The salary is very good, and he gets free board and lodging. It's a steady job and I hope he keeps it.'

Three days later Uncle Ken was on the veranda steps with his bedding roll and battered suitcase.

'Have you given up the hotel job?' asked Granny.

'No,' said Uncle Ken. 'They have closed down.'

'I hope it wasn't because of you.'

'No, Aunt Ellen. The bigger hotels in the hill stations are all closing down.'

'Well, never mind. Come along and have your tiffin. There is a *kofta* curry today. It's Ruskin's favourite.'

'Oh, is he here too? I have far too many nephews and nieces. Still he's preferable to those two girls of Mabel's. They made life miserable for me all the time I was with them in Simla.'

Over tiffin (as lunch was called in those days), Uncle Ken talked very seriously about ways and means of earning a living.

'There is only one taxi in the whole of Dehra,' he mused. 'Surely there is business for another?'*

'I'm sure there is,' said Granny. 'But where does it get you? In the first place, you don't have a taxi. And in the second place, you can't drive.'

---

* In the early 1940s Dehra had only one or two taxis. Today, there are over 500 plying in the town.

'I can soon learn. There's a driving school in town. And I can use Uncle's old car. It's been gathering dust in the garage for years.' (He was referring to Grandfather's vintage Hillman Roadster. It was a 1926 model: about twenty years old.)

'I don't think it will run now,' said Granny.

'Of course it will. It just needs some oiling and greasing and a spot of paint.'

'All right, learn to drive. Then we will see about the Roadster.'

So Uncle Ken joined the driving school.

He was very regular, going for his lessons for an hour in the evening. Granny paid the fee.

After a month Uncle Ken announced that he could drive and that he was taking the Roadster out for a trial run.

'You haven't got your licence yet,' said Granny.

'Oh, I won't take her far,' said Uncle Ken. 'Just down the road and back again.'

He spent all morning cleaning up the car. Granny gave him money for a can of petrol.

After tea Uncle Ken said, 'Come along, Ruskin, hop in and I will give you a ride. Bring Mohan along too.'

Mohan and I needed no urging. We got into the car beside Uncle Ken.

'Now don't go too fast, Ken,' said Granny anxiously. 'You are not used to the car as yet.'

Uncle Ken nodded and smiled and gave two sharp toots on the horn. He was feeling pleased with himself.

Driving through the gate, he nearly ran over Crazy.

Miss Kellner, coming out for her evening rickshaw ride, saw Uncle Ken at the wheel of the Roadster and went indoors again.

Uncle Ken drove straight and fast, tootling the horn without a break.

At the end of the road there was a roundabout.

'We'll turn here,' said Uncle Ken, 'and then drive back again.'

He turned the steering wheel; we began going round the roundabout; but the steering wheel wouldn't turn all the way, not as much as Uncle Ken would have liked it to . . . So, instead of going round, we took a right turn and kept going, straight on—and straight through the Maharaja of Jetpur's garden wall.

It was a single-brick wall, and the Roadster knocked it down and emerged on the other side without any damage to the car or any of its occupants. Uncle Ken brought it to a halt in the middle of the Maharaja's lawn.

Running across the grass came the Maharaja himself, flanked by his secretaries and their assistants.

When he saw that it was Uncle Ken at the wheel, the Maharaja beamed with pleasure.

'Delighted to see you, old chap!' he exclaimed. 'Jolly decent of you to drop in again. How about a game of tennis?'

**Uncle Ken at the Wicket**

Although restored to the Maharaja's favour, Uncle Ken was still without a job.

Granny refused to let him take the Hillman out again and so he decided to sulk. He said it was all Grandfather's fault for not seeing to the steering wheel ten years ago, while he was still alive. Uncle Ken went on a hunger strike for two hours (between tiffin and tea), and we did not hear him whistle for several days.

113

'The blessedness of silence,' said Granny.

And then he announced that he was going to Lucknow to stay with Aunt Emily.

'She has three children and a school to look after,' said Granny. 'Don't stay too long.'

'She doesn't mind how long I stay,' said Uncle Ken and off he went.

His visit to Lucknow was a memorable one, and we only heard about it much later.

When Uncle Ken got down at Lucknow station, he found himself surrounded by a large crowd, every one waving to him and shouting words of welcome in Hindi, Urdu and English. Before he could make out what it was all about, he was smothered by garlands of marigolds. A young man came forward and announced, 'The Gomti Cricketing Association welcomes you to the historical city of Lucknow,' and promptly led Uncle Ken out of the station to a waiting car.

It was only when the car drove into the sports' stadium that Uncle Ken realized that he was expected to play in a cricket match.

This is what had happened.

Bruce Hallam, the famous English cricketer, was touring India and had agreed to play in a charity match at Lucknow. But the previous evening, in Delhi, Bruce had gone to bed with an upset stomach and hadn't been able to get up in time to catch the train. A telegram was sent to the organizers of the match in Lucknow; but, like many a telegram, it did not reach its destination. The cricket fans of Lucknow had arrived at the station in droves to welcome the great cricketer. And by a strange coincidence, Uncle Ken

bore a startling resemblance to Bruce Hallam; even
the bald patch on the crown of his head was exactly
like Hallam's. Hence the muddle. And of course Uncle
Ken was always happy to enter into the spirit of a
muddle.

Having received from the Gomti Cricketing
Association a rousing reception and a magnificent
breakfast at the stadium, he felt that it would be
very unsporting on his part if he refused to play
cricket for them. 'If I can hit a tennis ball,' he mused,
'I ought to be able to hit a cricket ball.' And luckily
there was a blazer and a pair of white flannels in his
suitcase.

The Gomti team won the toss and decided to bat.
Uncle Ken was expected to go in at number three,
Bruce Hallam's normal position. And he soon found
himself walking to the wicket, wondering why on
earth no one had as yet invented a more comfortable
kind of pad.

The first ball he received was short-pitched, and
he was able to deal with it in tennis fashion, swatting
it to the mid-wicket boundary. He got no runs, but
the crowd cheered.

The next ball took Uncle Ken on the pad. He was
right in front of his wicket and should have been
given out lbw. But the umpire hesitated to raise his
finger. After all, hundreds of people had paid good
money to see Bruce Hallam play, and it would have
been a shame to disappoint them. 'Not out,' said the
umpire.

The third ball took the edge of Uncle Ken's bat
and sped through the slips.

'Lovely shot!' exclaimed an elderly gentleman in
the pavilion.

'A classic late cut,' said another.

The ball reached the boundary and Uncle Ken had four runs to his name. Then it was 'Over', and the other batsman had to face the bowling. He took a run off the first ball and called for a second run. Uncle Ken thought one run was more than enough. Why go charging up and down the wicket like a mad man? However, he couldn't refuse to run, and he was half-way down the pitch when the fielder's throw hit the wicket. Uncle Ken was run-out by yards. There could be no doubt about it this time.

He returned to the pavilion to the sympathetic applause of the crowd.

'Not his fault,' said the elderly gentleman. 'The other chap shouldn't have called. There wasn't a run there. Still, it was worth coming here all the way from Kanpur if only to see that superb late cut. . .'

\* \* \*

Uncle Ken enjoyed a hearty tiffin-lunch (taken at noon), and then, realizing that the Gomti team would probably have to be in the field for most of the afternoon—more running about!—he slipped out of the pavilion, left the stadium, and took a tonga to Aunt Emily's house in the cantonment.

He was just in time for a second lunch (taken at one o'clock) with Aunt Emily's family: and it was presumed at the stadium that Bruce Hallam had left early to catch the train to Allahabad, where he was expected to play in another charity match.

Aunt Emily, a forceful woman, fed Uncle Ken for a week, and then put him to work in the boys' dormitory of her school. It was several months before

116

he was able to save up enough money to run away and return to Granny's place.

But he had the satisfaction of knowing that he had helped the great Bruce Hallam to add another four runs to his grand aggregate. The scorebook of the Gomti Cricketing Association had recorded his feat for all time:

'B. Hallam run-out 4'

The Gomti team lost the match. But, as Uncle Ken would readily admit, where would we be without losers?

# The Typewriter

Working at nights in an attic room provided by my aunt, I took six months to complete my first book, a novel. I was eighteen at the time, and though the novel was about growing up in India, I was living in Jersey, in the Channel Islands, earning about four pounds a week as a Public Works' clerk.

I hadn't been away from India for as much as a year, but I was very homesick, and writing the book helped to take me back to the people and places I had known and loved.

Working in the same office was a sympathetic soul, a senior clerk whose name was Mr Bromley. He came from good Lancashire stock. His wife and son had predeceased him, and he lived alone in lodgings near the St Helier seafront. As I lived not far away, I would sometimes accompany Mr Bromley home after work, walking with him along the sea wall, watching the waves hissing along the sandy beaches or crashing against the rocks.

I gathered from some of his remarks that he had an incurable disease, and that he had come to live and work in Jersey in the hope that a sunnier climate would help him to get better. He did not tell me the nature of his illness; but he often spoke about his son, who had been killed in the War, and about the North Country, which was his home. He sensed that we were, in a way, both exiles, our real homes far from this small, rather impersonal island in the Channel.

He had read widely, and sympathized with my

ambitions to be a writer. He had tried it once himself, and failed.

'I didn't have the perseverance, lad' he said. 'I wasn't inventive enough, either. It isn't enough to be able to write well—you have to know how to tell a good story . . . Those who could do both, like Conrad and Stevenson, those are the ones we still read today. The critics keep telling us that Henry James was a master stylist, and so he was, but who reads Henry James?'

Mr Bromley rather admired my naïve but determined attempt to write a book.

On a Saturday afternoon I was standing in front of a shop, gazing wistfully at a baby portable typewriter on display. It was just what I wanted. My book was nearly finished but I knew I'd have to get it typed before submitting it to a publisher.

'Buying a typewriter, lad?' Mr Bromley had stopped beside me.

'I wish I could,' I said. 'But it's nineteen pounds and I've only got six pounds saved up. I'll have to hire some old machine.'

'But a good-looking typescript can make a world of difference, lad. Editors are jaded people. If they find a dirty manuscript on the desk, they feel like chucking it in the wastepaper basket—even if it is a masterpiece!'

'There's an old typewriter belonging to my aunt, but it should be in a museum. The letter b is missing. She must have used that one a lot—or perhaps it was my uncle. Anyway when I type my stories on it, I have to go through them again and ink in all the missing b's.'

'That won't do, lad. I tell you what, though. Give me your six pounds, and I'll add thirteen pounds to it, and we'll buy the machine. Then you can pay me back out of your wages—a pound every week. How would that suit you?'

I was both surprised and immensely thrilled. I had always thought Mr Bromley slightly stingy, as he seldom went to cinemas or restaurants. But here he was, offering to advance me the money for a new typewriter.

I accepted his offer and walked down the street in a state of happy euphoria, the gleaming new typewriter in my hand. I sat up late that night, hammering out the first chaper of my book.

It was midsummer then, and by the end of the year I had paid back six pounds to Mr Bromley. It was then that I received a letter from a publisher (the third to whom I had submitted the book) saying that they had liked my story but had some suggestions to make and could I call on them in London.

I took a few days' leave and crossed the Channel to England.

London swept me off my feet. The theatres and bookshops exerted their magic on me. And the publishers said they would take my book if only I'd try writing it again.

At eighteen, I was prepared to rewrite a book a dozen times, so I took a room in Hampstead, and grabbed the first job that came my way. I would have to keep working until I established myself as a writer. I did not know, then, how long this would take, but life was only just beginning, and I fell in love with someone, and someone fell in love with me, and both loves were unrequited, but all the same I was very happy.

For some time I did not send any money to Mr Bromley. My wage was modest, and London was expensive, and I wanted to enjoy myself a little. I meant to write to him, explaining the situation, but kept putting it off, telling myself that I would write as soon as I had some money to send him.

Several months passed. I wrote the book a third time, and this time it was accepted and I received a modest advance. I opened an account with Lloyd's, and then, finally, I made out a cheque in the name of Mr Bromley and mailed it to him with a letter.

But it was never to be cashed. It came back in the post with my letter, and along with it was a letter from my former employer saying that Mr Bromley had gone away and left no address. It seemed to me that he had given up his quest for better health, and had gone home to his own part of the country.

And so my debt was never paid.

The typewriter is still with me. I have used it for over thirty years, and it is now old and battered. But I will not give it away. It's like a guilty conscience, always beside me, always reminding me to pay my debts in time.

# IV

**MUSSOORIE SNAPSHOTS**

# In Search of John Lang

I had lived in Mussoorie just over four years without realizing that someone of literary distinction might be buried in the old English cemetery. Just as I was about to return to Delhi, a friend in Australia sent me a newspaper clipping which made mention of the first Australian-born novelist, John Lang, who spent the last years of his life in Mussoorie and was known to have been buried here. There is still an unsolved mystery about Lang's manuscripts. He left his papers to his second wife, nee Margaret Watter, but neither they, nor any trace of her after his death, have ever been found.

John Lang was born in Sydney in 1816. His father, a young soldier turned merchant, died before his birth. His mother was Elizabeth Harris, born on Norfolk Island, the daughter of two convicts. Lang proved a brilliant Latin scholar at Sydney College, then went to England to study law. He was expelled from Cambridge for *Botany Bay Tricks*—believed to be the writing of blasphemous litanies—but was admitted to the Society of the Middle Temple and called to the bar in 1841. He returned to Sydney shortly afterwards, but his convict connections stood in the way of his advancement, and it was only when he went to India that he began to lead a successful legal and literary life. *The Forger's Wife*—a robust tale of Australian outlaws—was published in England in 1855; *Botany Bay*—a collection of stories based on life in Sydney in the early years of the century—was written for Charles Dickens' magazine *Household Words* and published in 1859. The best of his books on India are *The Weatherbys* (1853) and *The Ex-Wife* (1859). These take a lightly satirical look at English social life in India, and are precursors of Kipling's stories of Simla society.*

Lang practiced at the Bar in Calcutta, and represented the Rani of Jhansi in her legal battles against the East India Company. He did well both as a barrister and as a newspaper proprietor. But none of his manuscripts, and no portrait of him, have ever been discovered. When he died he left everything to his second wife, whom he married in Mussoorie in 1861: but what happened to her after his death remains a mystery.

Although Lang's books are elusive, I decided that his grave should not be so hard to find, and set out in search of it on a crisp October morning. This is the best time of year in the hills, with the grass still fresh and green, the horse chestnut leaves yellowing, the hillsides sprinkled with wild geranium and umbrella-fronds of lady's lace.

I take the Camel's Back Road that leads round the northern and more forested face of Gun Hill, which is a rocky outcrop in the centre of the hill station. Gun Hill is so named because in Lang's time it boasted a cannon which boomed out at noon each day. The gun was a mixed blessing. Once on a Sunday morning during service in the Anglican Church of St Thomas (built in 1834 and now beginning to crumble), one of Fisher's straw cannon balls shot through the open door, bounced off a pew, and landed in the lap of a

---

* I have included one of his stories in *The Penguin Book of Indian Ghost Stories*.

stout lady who had been sleeping through the sermon.
Fisher was finally relieved of his job, and the cannon
was shifted to the municipal godowns where, for all I
know, it may still be gathering rust.

Although Mussoorie's Camel's Back Road was not
as high in social hierarchy as Scandal Point in Simla,
it was, until the 1930s, almost exclusively an European
preserve; and so was the cemetery, where most of the
names on the tombstones are of Anglo-Saxon vintage.
The graves occupy terraced slopes which face the
snow-covered Nilkanth and Bandarpoonchh ranges.

I am unable to enter at the gate which is securely
padlocked and encircled by barbed wire, making the
two large noticeboards—'No Trespassing' and 'Visitors
Should Leave Their Dogs Behind'—seem rather
unnecessary. I walk along the railing until I notice a
small footpath leading off the verge. Climbing over
the railings, I start down the path; but it is steep and
slippery with pine-needles, and I end by tobogganing
down the slope into a thicket of myrtle.

Brushing dust, burrs and pine-needles from my
clothes, I stand up and survey the hillside, my eyes
finally coming to rest on a small knoll where several
bulky obelisks rise from the ground. Obelisks were
all the rage in the late 19th century, and it is just
possible that John Lang's grave will be among them.

The knoll does seem to be the oldest part of the
cemetery; it is certainly the prettiest. The sunlight,
penetrating the gaps in the tall trees, plays chess on
the gravestones, shifting slowly and thoughtfully
across the worn old stones. The wind, like a hundred
violins, plays perpetually in the topmost branches of
the deodars. The only living thing in sight is an eagle,
wheeling high overhead. The snows are just a great

dazzle in the sky. This is a romantic spot, a fit burial ground for adventurers and pioneers. Here are the graves of soldiers, merchants, evangelists. The largest of the graves belongs to Mr Henry Bohle, who died in 1852. The financial benefits accruing to the hill station from Bohle's Brewery (now a ruin) led to Mackinnon going one better by building a cart road for his produce, and this road formed the basis for the present motor road from Dehra to Mussoorie.

There are a number of Mackinnons buried here. But unless John Lang left his widow in a generous mood, the chances of my finding his grave here are rather remote. Only the more expensive gravestones with marble insets have retained their inscriptions. The sandstone graves are now just anonymous slabs. Over a hundred monsoons have worn away the lettering on many old tombs.

I am still searching the knoll when I am hailed by a man holding a bundle of sticks in one hand and an axe in the other. He calls out to me in a belligerent tone:

'What are you doing here? And how did you get in?'

'I am looking for a grave,' I reply mildly.

'You may come across your own grave if you walk in here without permission!'

This must be the mali, who is both gardener and caretaker. I have been warned about him; a fierce man who has been known to eject intruders at the point of a lathi. I am told he is short-sighted; and, like a bear, which is also short-sighted, believes that there is no point in trying to identify an intruder until he has been finished off.

It is only when the mali comes closer, and finds that I look fairly respectable, that his bluster disappears.

'Some people come here to rob the graves,' he explains in an injured tone. 'And every time an arm or a head or a piece of marble goes,' he says, gesturing towards a decapitated angel, 'the Committee-memsahibs take me to task for carelessness.'

'Well, I'll tell the memsahibs how vigilant you are. I am looking for an old grave. Over a hundred years old.'

'There are some old ones near my house,' he says, beginning to mellow. 'But you should look at the register, sahib. That will help you find your relative's grave.'

I am about to tell him that it is not a relative's grave, then decide not to as I do not want to raise his suspicions again. And it is pleasant to invent a relationship with another writer, a fellow Indo-Anglian, who lived, loved, died and was buried here over a hundred years ago.

'Who has the register?'

'The Garlah miss-sahib. She will tell you everything.'

'All right, I'll see her and come again tomorrow.'

'If you bring a chit from the miss-sahib, I can open the gate for you.'

I continue searching on my own for a while, to the evident unease of the mali. Does he really think I shall make off with a headstone?

That evening I visit Miss Garlah. She is a tubby little Anglo-Indian lady with a hearty manner and a strong constitution. Forty of her sixty years have been spent in Mussoorie.

'Did you have trouble with the mali?' she asks with apparent relish. Evidently she looks forward to getting complaints about him.

'He was a bit aggressive,' I say. 'He needs glasses to help him separate grave robbers from other people.'

'Well, he saw you climbing the railings, and that made him wonder what you were up to.'

'So he's been to you already?'

'Yes, he's very good. We keep him because he's so tough. The last man used to let in all sorts of people, including some hippies who thought the cemetery would be just the right place for smoking pot.'

When I tell her the object of my search, she says: 'Yes, I have a register. Give me the name and date of your author's death and we'll look him up.'

'John Lang, 1864.'

'Ah, that's going too far back. There must have been a register for those years, but if there was, it's long since lost. I can help you from 1910 onwards.'

I make no attempt to hide my disappointment. 'Nothing earlier? If only I had an idea of where the grave might be situated, I might be able to identify it.'

'Well, young man, I can only suggest that you keep hunting. Try the graves near the mail's house. I'll ask him to clean them up for you. You may be lucky. We do our best to maintain them because the British High Commission makes us a small grant towards their upkeep. But we're short-handed, and the heavy monsoon rains don't help.'

The next day I am back at the cemetery, determined to make one more attempt at finding John Lang's grave. I am leaving for Delhi in a day or two, and it may be months, perhaps years, before I can return to Mussoorie.

This time I find the gate open. A small boy with

little on goes skipping over the graves, like some mischievous cupid trying to resurrect dead lovers. His father, the mali, appears from behind a placid buffalo and gives me an elaborate salaam. Apparently Miss Garlah has already sent word of my coming.

The mali apologizes for the condition of some of the graves near his outhouse. His buffalo is tethered to a crumbling obelisk. A cow and calf are tied to a slanting stone cross. Several graves are half-buried under straw and offal. Others appear to have vanished into a small ploughed field which now contains mustard. The strangest sight of all is a memorial tablet, commemorating a certain Captain Jones of Her Majesty's 30th Foot, which lies flat on the step of the mali's shack and provides an ideal platform for the gardener's tall and ornate hookah pipe.

The chances of finding John Lang's grave in this tumbled, crumbling heap now seem remote. But the mali offers to help me in my search and he is so anxious to please that I am loath to disappoint him. He starts scraping the mud off partly obscured inscriptions and tells his small son, a merry little fellow with bright eyes and a disarming smile, to do the same. It is a glorious day, but the wind is from behind the mali's house, and there is no escape from the odour of sour milk and cow dung. I came in search of the dead, only to find the living.

We find several graves dating from 1864 and earlier, but John Lang's is not one of them. I begin to harbour mean thoughts about his wife. If she could disappear so suddenly and mysteriously with his manuscripts, it is unlikely that she would have bothered to give him an expensive and permanent grave.

'There were a few on this northern slope, sahib.' says the mali after some time, 'but we had a landslide a few years ago and the graves went down the khud.'

This is enough to make me give up all hope. For all I know, John Lang's remains may well be at the foot of the mountain. My search becomes desultory, and I find myself muttering, 'What does it matter, anyway? If a writer's any good, his books will be his monument. What need have we of tombstones to commemorate our passage on earth?'

But all the same I am disappointed. And seeing my disappointment, the mali makes renewed efforts to clean up some of the graves near the cattle shed. He cannot understand my whim, or anyone's sentimentality over old graves, but he has warmed towards me, wants to please me, and would be quite willing to chisel 'John Lang, died 1864' into any grave I choose, if it will make me happy.

Three weeks after leaving Mussoorie, I receive a letter from Miss Garlah, informing me that the old register had turned up and that John Lang had indeed been buried in the Mussoorie cemetery, on 'C' terrace.

On a subsequent visit I made my way to the spot and found the grave quite easily, under a covering of moss and ferns; shaded by the deodars, it was just a mound of earth and foliage. Prem and I cleared away a hundred years of detritus, and there on a plain stone slab was the simple inscription—'John Lang, Barrister at law. Died Landour, 1864, aged 47.'

# The Himalaya Club

## *(by John Lang)*

*(This extract from a piece by John Lang published in Charles Dickens' weekly journal,* Household Words, *paints a charming picture of life in Mussoorie in the 1850s.)*

It is some eighteen years since this institution was founded, at Mussoorie, one of the chief sanataria in the Himalaya Mountains. Here all those who can obtain leave, and who can afford the additional expense, repair to escape the hot weather of the plains. The season begins about the end of April, and ends about the first week in October. The club is open to the members of the civil and military services, to the members of the Bar, the clergy, and to such other private gentlemen who are on the government house list, which signifies 'in society'. The club-house is neither an expensive nor an elegant edifice, but it answers the purposes required of it. It has two large rooms, one on the ground floor, and the other on the upper storey. The lower room, which is some sixty feet long by twenty-five wide, is the dining room. The upper room is the reading and the ball room. The club has also its billiard room, which is built on the ledge of a precipice, and its stables, which would astonish most persons in Europe. No horses, except those educated in India, would crawl into these holes cut out of the earth and rock.

Facing the side door is a platform about forty yards long by fifteen feet wide; and from it, on a clear day, the eye commands one of the grandest scenes in the known world. In the distance are plainly visible the eternal snows; at your feet are a number of hills, covered with trees of luxuriant foliage. Amongst them is the rhododendron, which grows to an immense height and size, and is, when in bloom, literally covered with flowers. On every hill, on a level with the club, and within a mile of it, a house is to be seen, to which access would seem impossible. These houses are, for the most part, whitened without as well as within; and nothing can exceed in prettiness their aspect as they shine in the sun.

From the back of the club-house—from your bedroom windows (there are twenty-three sets of apartments) you have a view of Deyrah Dhoon. It appears about a mile off. It is seven miles distant. The plains that lie outstretched below the Simplon bear, in point of extent and beauty, to the Indian scene nothing like the proportion which the comparatively pigmy Mont Blanc bears to the Dewalgiri. From an elevation of about seven thousand feet the eye embraces a plain containing millions of acres, intersected by broad streams to the left, and inclosed by a low belt of hills, called the Pass. The Dhoon, in various parts, is dotted with clumps of jungle, abounding with tigers, pheasants, and every species of game. In the broad tributaries to the Ganges and the Jumna may be caught (with a fly) the mahseer, the leviathan salmon. Beyond the Pass of which I have spoken, you see the plains of Hindoostan. While you are wrapped in a great coat, and are shivering with the cold, you may see the heat, and the steam it occasions. With us on the hills, the themometer is at forty-five; with those poor fellows over there, it is at ninety-two degrees. We can scarcely keep ourselves warm, for the wind comes from the snowy range; they cannot breathe, except beneath a punkah. That steam is, as the crow files, not more than forty miles from us.

We are all idlers at Mussoorie. We are all sick, or supposed to be so; or we have leave on private affairs. Some of us are up here for a month between musters. We are in the good graces of our colonel, and our general—the general of our division, a very good old gentleman.

Let us go into the public room, and have breakfast; for, it is half past nine o' clock, and the bell has rung. There are not more than half-a-dozen at the table. There are the early risers who walk or ride round the Camel's Back every morning; the Camel's Back being a huge mountain, encircled about its middle by a good road. The majority of the club's members are asleep, and will defer breakfast until tiffin time—half past two. At that hour the gathering will be great. How these early risers eat to be sure! There is the Major, who, if you believe him, has every complaint mentioned in *Graham's Domestic Medicine*, has just devoured two thighs (grilled) of a turkey, and is now asking Captain Blossom's opinion of the Irish stew, while he's cutting into a pigeon pie.

Let us now while away the morning. Let us call on some of the grass widows. There are lots of them here, civil and military. Let us go first to Mrs Merrydale, the wife of our old friend Charley, of the two hundred and tenth regiment. Poor fellow! He could not get leave, and the doctors said another hot summer in the plains would be the death of his wife. They are seven hundred pounds in debt to the Agra bank, and are hard put to it to live and pay the monthly instalments of interest. Charley is only a lieutenant. What terrible infants are these little Merrydales! There is Lieutenant Maxwell's pony under the trees, and if these children had not shouted out 'Mamma! Mamma! Here is Captain Wall Sahib!' I should have been informed that Mrs Merrydale was not at home, or was poorly, which I should have believed implicitly. (Maxwell, when a young ensign, was once engaged to be married to Julia Dacey, now Mrs Merrydale, but her parents would not hear of it, for some reason or other.) As it is, we must be admitted. We will not stay long. Mrs Merrydale is writing to her huband. Grass widows in the hills are always writing to their husbands when you drop in upon them, and your presence is not actually delighted in. How beautiful she looks! now that the mountain breezes have chased from her cheeks the pallor which lately clung to them in the plains; and the fresh air has imparted to her spirits an elasticity, in lieu of that langour by which she was oppressed a fortnight ago.

Let us now go to Mrs Hastings. She is the wife of a civilian, who has a salary of fifteen hundred rupees (one hundred and fifty pounds) per mensem, and who is a man of fortune, independent of his pay. Mrs Hastings has the best house in Mussoorie. She is surrounded by servants. She has no less than three Arab horses to ride. She is a great prude—is Mrs Hastings. She has no patience with married women who flirt. She thinks that the dogma—

'When lovely women go astray.

Their stars are more in fault than they'—
is all nonsense. Mrs Hastings has been a remarkably fine woman; she is now five-and-thirty, and still good-looking, though disposed to embonpoint. She wearies one with her discourses on the duties of a wife. That

simpering cornet, Stammersleigh, is announced, and we may bid her good morning.

The average rent for a furnished house is about five hundred rupees (fifty pounds) for the six months. Every house has its name. Yonder are Cocky Hall, Belvidere, Phoenix Lodge, the Cliffs, the Crags, the Vale, the Eagle's Nest, & c. The value of these properties ranges from five hundred to fifteen hundred pounds. The furniture is of the very plainest description, with one or two exceptions, and is manufactured chiefly at Bareilly, and carried here on men's shoulders, the entire distance—ninety miles.

Where shall we go now, for it wants an hour to tiffin time? Oh! here comes a janpan! (a sort of sedan-chair carried by four hillmen dressed in loose black clothes turned up with red, yellow, blue, green or whatever colour the proprietor likes best.) And in the janpan sits a lady—Mrs Apsley, a very pretty, good-tempered, and well-bred little woman. She is the grand-daughter of an English peer, and is very fond of quoting her aunts and her uncles. 'My aunt Lady Mary Culnerson,' 'my uncle, Lord Charles Banbury Cross, &c.' But that is her only weakness, I believe; and, perhaps, it is ungenerous to allude to it. Her husband is in the Dragoons.

'Well, Mrs Apsley, whither art thou going? To pay visits?'

'No, I am going to Mrs Ludlam's to buy a new bonnet, and not before I want one you will say.'

'May I accompany you?'

'Yes, and assist me in making a choice.'

There is not a cloud to be seen. The air is soft and balmy. The wild flowers are in full bloom, and the butterfly is on the wing. The grasshopper is singing his ceaseless song, and the bees are humming a chorus thereto.

We are now at Mrs Ludlam's. The janpan is placed upon the ground, and I assist Mrs Apsley to step from it.

Mrs Ludlam is the milliner and dressmaker of Upper India, and imports all her wares direct from London and Paris. Everybody in this part of the world knows Mrs Ludlam, and everybody likes her. She has by industry, honesty of purpose, and economy, amassed a little fortune; and has brought up a large family in the most respectable and unpretending style. Some people say that she sometimes can afford to sell a poor ensign's wife a bonnet, or a silk dress, at a price which hardly pays. What I have always admired in Mrs Ludlam is that she never importunes her customers to buy her goods; nor does she puff their quality.

The bonnet is bought; likewise a neckscarf for Jack. And we are now returning: Mrs Apsley to her home, and I to the club. Mrs Apsley invites me to dine with them; but that is impossible. It is public night, and I have two guests. One of them is Jack, who does not belong to the club, because Mary does not wish it.

Mrs Apsley says she wants some pickles, and we must go into Ford's shop to purchase them. Ford sells everything; and he is a wine, beer, and spirit merchant. You may get anything at Ford's—guns, pistols, swords, whips, hats, clothes, tea, sugar, tobacco. What is this which Ford puts into my hand? A raffle paper! 'To be raffled for a single-barrelled rifle by Purdy. The property of a gentleman hard-up for money, and in great difficulties. Twenty-five chances at one gold mohur (one pound twelve shillings) each.'

'Yes, put my name down for a chance, Ford.'

'And Captain Apsley's, please,' says the lady.

After promising Mrs Apsley, most faithfully, that I will not keep Jack later than half-past twelve, and taking another look into those sweet eyes of hers, I gallop away as fast as the pony can carry me. I am late; there is scarcely a vacant place at the long table. We have no private tables. The same board shelters the nether limbs of all of us. We are all intimate friends, and know exactly each other's circumstances. What a clatter of knives and forks! And what a lively conversation! It alludes, chiefly, to the doings of the past night. Almost every other man has a nickname. To account for many of them would indeed be a difficult, if not a hopeless task.

'Dickey Brown! Glass of beer?'

'I am your man,' responds Major George, N.I. Fencibles.

At the other end of the table you hear the word 'Shiney' shouted out, and responded to by Lieutenant Fenwick of the Horse Artillery.

'Billy! Sherry?'

Adolphus Bruce of the Lancers lifts his glass with immense alacrity.

It is a curious characteristic of Indian society that very little outward respect is in private shown to seniority. I once heard an ensign of twenty years of age address a civilian of sixty in the following terms: 'Now then, old moonsiff, pass that claret, please.'

# Mukesh's Brush with the Art World

My artist friends don't talk to me any more, and presently I'll tell you why.

Over the years I've known a number of artists, some of them big names now, some not so big, but almost all of them the possessors of very large egos. I have come across a few temperamental musicians, as well as a fair number of conceited writers and journalists, but when it comes to the vanity stakes, the artists are way ahead! Each one fancies himself another Picasso or Modigliani or Jamini Roy.

Well, in the days when I could afford such frivolities, I sometimes bought the odd painting. I wouldn't call any of them an investment, because up to now no one has offered to take them off my hands even at throwaway prices. I have had offers for the frames but not for the paintings. Some of these works of art were originally given to me—you might call them 'gallery rejects'.

On at least two occasions I had hired galleries in New Delhi to help promote the work of budding new artists. (You could at least get a cup of tea near the Shankar Market gallery; not so at the AIFACS, at least not in those days.) Helping the artists explain their work to puzzled visitors did nothing for my own credibility. Even so, we sold a couple of pictures.

Inspired by this success, one of the artists wisely went into the garment business. The other, even more sensible, did a Paul Gauguin in reverse and became a successful stockbroker in Boston.

Over the years I have accumulated an odd assortment of paintings, so much so that now there is no space in my small godown for other more useful things such as gardening tools, battered bicycles, stove pipes and broken chairs. Juxtaposed, these items would in themselves make an interesting exhibition of modern art, but they are not paintings.

Included in this collection of undisplayable art was a small portrait in oils done of this writer by an itinerant artist who can only be described as a 'gifted amateur'. I can't bear to hurt anyone's feelings, but the children in my household have no such qualms. Commenting on the portrait, one of them said I looked like a poached egg; the other, that I resembled a well-known film star bereft of his wig; and the third, that I looked like Queen Victoria on a postage stamp. I was about to toss the painting into the fire when thirteen-year-old Mukesh, who does a little brushwork for fun, told me he would improve upon it.

And he did, too. A thick coating of daffodil-yellow removed my face from the picture, leaving only the outline of my spectacles and double chin. He then turned my specs into bicycle wheels and my chin into a watermelon. A duck, two roosters and a pink pig were introduced into the picture, so that the end result was a jolly rural scene. The picture went up on my sitting room wall. Fortunately for my safety, the original artist now lives in Bangkok, where he paints murals for massage parlours.

It now occurred to us that some of the other paintings in the godown would benefit from Mukesh's methods. There was one in particular that I strongly resented. It showed a woman in a reclining posture; she had a very small head but very long legs. I have never known a woman with such long legs. One of them could have been substituted for the neck of a giraffe. Don't artists keep mistresses any more? Or perhaps the artist's model had been a *churel*, able to elongate her arms and legs at will.

Mukesh and I scraped off the dirt and set about restoring the painting. He shortened the woman's legs to the acceptable length, and gave her an Afro hairstyle to correct the proportions of her head. Her sari, a dirty white, was changed to petunia-pink, and an empty window was brightened up by the introduction of a bright green parrot.

This masterpiece also went up on the sitting room wall!

Here it was soon joined by several others, now much more colourful and in tune with the natural world. Casual visitors (one of them an art critic) went into raptures over some of the paintings.

And then, last week, who should walk into our flat but 'Matisse' himself, the creator and only begetter of the lady with the serpentine legs.

I was hoping he wouldn't recognize his old painting, but Mukesh had forgotten to remove the original signature. 'Matisse' looked at it once, he looked at it a second time. At the third inspection he resembled a Pekinese whose eyeballs have parted from their sockets.

He barged out of the sitting room, tumbled down the stairs, and went rushing down the road telling everyone he met that I was the most treacherous person on earth. Mukesh later saw him at Dr Bisht's clinic, having his blood pressure checked.

Since then he has been seen to come out of bookshops, arms laden with copies of my books, which he proceeds to tear apart and stamp on in the street. At least my sales are going up.

# The Box Man

Sitting outside my cottage, in the summer shade of an old plum tree, I can see a path leading through the deodars towards the next tree-darkened mountain. On this morning, I saw an old man coming down the path, walking very slowly, carrying a small tin trunk on his head.

He stopped at the gate and asked me if I would buy something. I could think of nothing I wanted, but the old man looked so tired, so very old, that I thought he would collapse if he moved any further along the path without resting. So I asked him to step in and show me his wares. He had a snow-white beard, crinkled brown skin, and bright intelligent eyes. He was thin and bandy-legged and wore a patched, black waistcoat.

He couldn't get the box off his head by himself, but together we managed to set it down in the shade and the old man insisted on spreading the entire contents out on the grass: bangles, combs, shoe-laces, safety-pins, cheap stationery, buttons, pomades, elastic, and scores of other minor household necessities.

When I refused buttons because there was no one to sew them on for me, he plied me with safety-pins. I said no; but, as he moved from article to article, his querulous, persuasive voice slowly broke down my sales resistance, and I ended up buying envelopes, a letter-pad (pink roses on bright blue paper), a one-rupee fountain-pen, and several yards of elastic. I had no idea what I would use the elastic for, but the old man convinced me that I could no longer live without it.

He then produced a small plastic glass from his waistcoat pocket, and I thought it was another item for sale. But he only wanted a drink of water. I readily brought him some. He drank the water slowly, then leant back against the trunk of the plum tree, making no effort to pack his things. He closed his eyes. I had a suden panicky feeling that he would die in my garden!

'I am very tired, hazoor,' he said. 'Please do not mind if I rest here for a while.' 'Rest for as long as you like,' I said. 'That's a heavy load to carry on a hot day.' He opened his eyes at the chance of a conversation and said, 'When I was a young man, it was nothing. I could cary my box up from Rajpur to Mussoorie by the bridle-path—seven steep miles! But now I find it difficult to cover even one mile from the bazar to the Mall.'

'Naturally, you are old.' 'Seventy years old, sahib.' 'You are very fit for your age. You do not look more than sixty-five.' Though he was frail, he had a wiry frame and his skin still had a healthy colour. 'Don't you have anyone to help you?' I asked.

'I had a boy last month, but he stole my earnings and ran off to *Dilli*. I wish my son was alive—he would not have permitted me to work like a mule for a living. But he died five years ago, of a cough.' By a 'cough', I presume, he meant tuberculosis. 'Have you no relatives, then?' 'None. I have outlived them all. That is the curse of a healthy life. Your friends, your loved ones, all go before you and at the end you are left alone. But I must go too, before long. The road seems more difficult each day. I feel as though it has added a mile to its length. The stones are harder. The sun is hotter. Even some of the trees that were here in my

145

youth have grown old and died. I have outlived the trees.'

He had outlived the trees. And I was certain that if he fell asleep in my garden he would strike root there, sending out crooked branches. I could imagine a small bent tree with a black waistcoat. He closed his eyes again, but kept on talking.

'Yes, there were times when the memsahibs bought great quantities of elastic. Today it is ribbons and bangles for the girls, and combs for the boys. But I do not make so much. Not because people do not buy from me, but because I cannot walk as far. How many houses do I reach in a day? Ten, fifteen. But twenty years ago I could walk to fifty houses. That makes a difference.'

'Have you always been here?'

'Most of my life, hazoor. Except when I went to Najibabad to get married. I was here before they built the motor road, when gentlemen came up on ponies, and their women in dandies borne by coolies. I was cinemas I was here when the Prince of *Welles* came from across the sea. And I was here during the earthquake—when that was, I cannot remember exactly, I was only a boy—but the hills shook and many houses fell. Oh, I have been here a long time, hazoor. I was here when this house was built. Fifty, sixty years ago, it must have been. I cannot remember exactly. What is ten years when you have lived seventy? It was a Major Sahib who built your house. I remember, because he did not live in it for long. He was thrown from his horse one day, and was killed. Then came—I forget the name—and his wife and children. Beautiful children. But they went away many years ago. Everyone has gone away.'

'But others have come,' I said. 'True, and that is as it should be. That is not my complaint. My complaint is that I have been left behind.' He produced his little glass again. 'I am sorry, hazoor, but talking has made me thirsty.'

I took the glass and went indoors to fill it. By the time I returned to the garden the old man had miraculously put away all his odds and ends. He stood over his old blue tin box, gazing down at it with a mixture of disdain and affection.

I helped him lift it, and placed it on the flattened cloth on his head. I opened the gate, and the box man tottered out. He did not have the energy to turn and make a salutation of any kind; but, setting his sights on the mountain ahead, he walked up the path with steps that were shaky and slow but wonderfully straight.

I watched him until he was far along the path. I wondered how long he could last. Perhaps a year or two, perhaps a day, pehaps an hour. But whenever or however he died, it wouldn't be death. He was too old to die. He could only sleep. He could only fall gently, like an old brown leaf.

# Ghosts of the Savoy

The clock over the Savoy Bar is stationary at 8.20 and has been like that since the atomic bomb was dropped on Hiroshima fifty years ago. That's what Nandu tells me, and I have no reason to disbelieve him. Many of his more outlandish statements often turn out to be true.

Almost any story about this old hotel in Mussoorie has a touch of the improbable about it, even when supported by facts. A previous owner, Mr McClintock, had a false nose—according to Nandu, who never saw it. So I checked with old Negi, who first came to work in the hotel as a room boy back in 1932 (a couple of years before I was born) and who, sixty years and two wives later, looks after the front office. Negi tells me it's quite true.

'I used to take McClintock sahib his cup of cocoa last thing at night. After leaving his room I'd dash around to one of the windows and watch him until he went to bed. The last thing he did, before putting the light out, was to remove his false nose and place it on the bedside table. He never slept with it on. I suppose it bothered him whenever he turned over or slept on his face. First thing in the morning, before having his cup of tea, he'd put it on again. A great man, McClintock sahib.'

'But how did he lose his nose in the first place?' I asked.

'Wife bit it off,' said Nandu.

'No, sir,' said Negi, whose reputation for telling the truth is proverbial. 'It was shot away by a German bullet during World War I. He got the Victoria Cross as compensation.'

'And when he died, was he wearing his nose?' I asked.

'No, sir,' said old Negi, continuing his tale with some relish. 'One morning when I took the sahib his cup of tea, I found him stone dead, *without his nose!* It was lying on the bedside table. I suppose I should have left it there, but McClintock sahib was a good man, I could not bear to have the whole world knowing about his false nose. So I stuck it back on his face and then went and informed the manager. A natural death, just a sudden heart attack. But I made sure that he went into his coffin with his nose attached!'

We all agreed that Negi was a good man to have around, especially in a crisis.

Mr McClintock's ghost is supposed to haunt the corridors of the hotel, but I have yet to encounter it. Will the ghost be wearing its nose? Old Negi thinks not (the false nose being man-made), but then he hasn't seen the ghost at close quarters, only receding into the distance between the two giant deodars on the edge of the Beer Garden. Those deodars have been there a couple of hundred years—before the hotel was built, before the hill station came up.

* * *

A lot of people who enter the Bar look pretty far gone, and sometimes I have difficulty distinguishing the living from the dead. But the real ghosts are those who manage to slip away without paying for their drinks.

I don't have to slip away. In the five or six years during which I have helped to prop up the Savoy Bar, I have seldom paid for a drink. That's the kind of friend I have in Nandu. You won't find a harsh word about him in these pages. I think he decided long ago that I was an adornment to the Bar, and that, draped over a bar stool, I looked like Ray Milland in *The Lost Weekend*. (He won an Oscar for that, remember?)

As for the Man-from-Sail, who is usually parked on the next bar stool, he's no adornment, in spite of the Jackie Shroff-moustache. But I have to admit that he's skilful at pouring drinks, mixing cocktails and showing tipsy ladies to the powder room. He doesn't pay for his drinks either.

How, then, does dear Nandu survive? Obviously there are some real customers in the wings, and we help them feel at home, chatting them up and encouraging them to try the Royal Salute or even a glass of Beaujolais. I can rattle off the history of the hotel for anyone who wants to hear it; and as for the Man-from-Sail, he provides a free ambulance service for those who can't handle the hotel's hospitality. The Man-from-Sail is the town's number one blood donor, so if you come away from your transfusion with a bad hangover, you'll know whose blood is coursing around in your veins. But it's real Scotch, not the stuff they make at the bottom of the Sail mountain.

Nandu tells me that Pearl Buck, the Nobel laureate, stayed here for a few days in the early fifties. I looked up the hotel register and found that he was right as usual. As far as I know, Miss Buck did not record her impressions of the hotel or the town in any of her books. It's the sort of place people usually have something to say about. Like the correspondent of the

*Melbourne Age* who complained because the roof had blown off his room during one of our equinoxal storms. A frivolous sort of complaint, to say the least. Nandu placated him by saying, 'Sir, in Delhi you can only get a five-star room. From your room here you can see *all* the stars!' And so he could, once the clouds had rolled away.

It's a windy sort of mountain, and in cyclonic storms our corrugated iron roofs are frequently blown away. Old Negi recalls that a portion of the Savoy roof once landed on the St George's School flat, five miles away, at the height of the midsummer storm. In its flight it decapitated an early-morning fitness freak. Had anyone else told me the story, I wouldn't have believed it. But Negi's word is the real thing—as good as a sip of Johnie Walker Blue Label.

\* \* \*

And here's a limerick I wrote for Nandu and the Man-from-Sail:

> There was a young man who could fix
> Anything in five minutes or six;
> His statue is found
> On Savoy's hallowed ground,
> With Nandu beside him, transfix'd!

# Bear in the Ballroom

The Old Savoy Bar has witnessed the passage of many famous celebrities—film stars, politicians, business tycoons, beauty queens—and sometimes they merge into one composite personality, vanity being the common factor. But the most unusual visitor was the brown Himalayan bear who wandered into the hotel after a heavy snowfall last January. During severe winters, when food is scarce, wild animals occasionally wander into the hill station—remember the leopard that carried off all the Landour strays a couple of years ago?

I was sitting on my favourite bar stool (the one that tilts slightly) waiting for the Man-from-Sail to walk in and sign for my drink, when I heard the swing-door open behind me. Without bothering to look around, I said, 'Come on, old chap, you're half an hour late this evening.'

All I got in response was a grunt. Now, the Man-from-Sail does snore (I have shared a railway compartment with him), but I have never known him to snore standing up.

'In a bad mood?' I asked, and knocking on the counter to attract the attention of the barman, said, 'Get Sail sahib a whisky-and-soda.' The barman came out from behind his cubby hole, looked over my shoulder, and let out a shrill cry, rather in the manner of a wounded stag.

I turned then, and saw the bear a few feet away, looking very hairy and threatening. Did I ever tell you that I was the 200-metres hurdles champion in my school days? Well, I can assure you that at sixty I've lost none of my speed or skill. I was over the bar counter like lightning, holding hands with the barman, a nice boy but not my type.

The bear was now separated from us by the high counter, and not being a high hurdler itself, began to vent its frustration by flinging bar stools all over the place. With great presence of mind the barman shook himself free of my embrace, picked up the house phone and rang the front office. Almost immediately he got Nandu on the line, and the conversation went something like this:

Prakash : 'Sir, there's a bear in the bar.'

Nandu: 'Make sure you give him a bill.'

Prakash: 'A bear, sir, not a customer.'

Nandu: 'A bare customer? Did he have too much to drink?'

Prakash: 'No, sir. Bear—big *bhaloo*, brown bear!'

Nandu: 'Well, give Mr Bayer a drink and ask Mr Bond to look after him till I get there. He's here to arrange a conference. Bayer and Bayer, you know. They're into cosmetics. Very important customer.' Nandu put the phone down and we were left to our own devices.

The bear had now discovered a decorated Christmas tree in a corner of the room and was proceeding to take it apart. Paper streamers, tinsel stars and imitation plastic holly were soon festooned over the rampant animal. While this mayhem was still in progress, Nandu and the Man-from-Sail entered at the swing-doors. Bravehearts both, they backed out again and ran for the security guard. It was the first time I'd seen the Man-from-Sail at a loss for words.

The security guard (a retired Havaldar from

Meerut) carried a muzzle-loader which dated back to the Mutiny. He rushed into the room and fired at random, shattering the glass of the clock that had been stationary ever since the atom bomb fell on Hiroshima. The hands now made rapid and seemingly endless revolutions, as though to make up for all the lost years when time stood still.

The bear rushed at the security guard, who left by the swing-doors and retreated to the conference room where Nandu and the Man-from-Sail were holding a council-of-war. Fortunately for Prakash and me, the bear was able to negotiate the doors, and finding the lobby deserted, made off down the corridor, stopping at the only occupied room on the ground floor. In residence was Miss Darshini Singh, an up-and-coming TV producer who was planning to film some of my plain tales from the hills.

Miss Darshini had only just arrived from Chennai, where she had been making a documentary on crocodiles. She was still wearing the Crocodile Dundee hat that had been presented to her by an elderly Australian tourist. After crocodiles, bear were small fry to her. When the Savoy bear thudded into the door of her room, she flung open the door, clapped her hands in delight, and exclaimed, 'Oh, how cute! A real live bear! The Man-from-Sail must have arranged it. He really is enterprising. Now we can fix that scene in which the bear chases Ruskin Bond up a maple tree!'

Miss Darshini's dog Rambo, an overfed golden retriever of considerable charm and no character, now rushed at the door, barking furiously. Bears are afraid of barking dogs; they don't know what to make of them. The visiting bear turned and continued its journey down the corridors of the Savoy until it found the billiard room.

'Oh, no, not my billiard cloth!' cried Nandu in genuine distress. 'It cost me a fortune! Made in Holland, 1922. Of course I'm not that old,' he added, as an afterthought.

Fortunately the bear went past the billiard room, dashing instead into the old ballroom which was sometimes used for conferences and dinner parties. The annual State Bank party was in progress, with the Commissioner as Chief Guest. He was deep in conversation with Hugh and Colleen Gantzer, the travel writers, who had just returned from Alaska— or was it Madagascar? No respecter of persons, the bear charged straight through the gathering of dignitaries, upsetting a drinks cart, two waiters and the Commissioner's tipsy wife. Then, entangled in a tablecloth ('Don't forget to bill them for it,' cried Nandu), the uninvited guest dashed off into the night, heading in the direction of Convent Hill. But that's a nun's story.

# A Handful of Nuts

On a wet and windy night, I was sitting at the Savoy Bar, warming my feet with the memory of old fires (firewood being scarce and expensive), when in walked the Man-from-Sail, shaking snowflakes and dandruff from his coat.

He was followed, minutes later, by Heaven-Born the actor and Heaven-Sent the publisher, both well-preserved men in their late fifties. Great buddies, both of them, even though they occasionally came to blows. Their wives had better things to do than prop up the Savoy Bar. Heaven-Sent usually had one or two ex-Cabinet Ministers in tow (he owned a newspaper at the time) but on this occasion he was mercifully free of his entourage. Heaven-Born had left his purple robe at home (you can see it in the famous picture taken by the Man-from-Sail), which meant that he was wearing the off-white summer suit that he had worn to such effect in his last big hit.

Heaven-Born had this wonderful idea for a period movie set in the Savoy, which of course was the ideal place for a *Far Pavilion*-type epic. Heaven-Born was to act and direct, while the Man-from-Sail, who is something of an all-rounder, was to help with the script, the casting, the props, the catering, the still photography and the make-up. Nandu and I were offered bit parts as decadent nawabs. Heaven-Sent was to provide the financial backing. Or at least that was the idea.

Nandu wasn't too happy about the whole thing, especially as the climax of the film (as envisaged in the script) showed the hotel going up in flames. The old hotel with its rhododendron beams, pinewood panelling, walnut wood doors and deodar floorboards, was really quite vulnerable, and it wouldn't have taken much to turn a 'studio' fire into the real thing.

'You're insured, aren't you?' said Heaven-Born, determined to override Nandu's protests. 'Or we could use a model,' he added.

'Your house should do,' said Nandu, 'it's small enough for a model.'

I steered the conversation away from arson and incendiaries to the traditional Savoy Queen dinner-and-dance held every summer. Next year's winner was to receive a free trip to Uzbekistan, one way only. Nandu asked Heaven-Born if he would like to officiate as a judge for the beauty contests and he graciously consented.

Heaven-Sent felt that there should be several judges, and more names were proposed—Tom Alter, Prem Chopra, Hugh and Colleen Gantzer, Prince This and Princess That, Khushwant Singh and Sunderlal Bahuguna. Heaven-Born looked a little put out and said he thought he could manage without so much help. Heaven-Sent then proposed the name of one of his ex-Cabinet Ministers. I suggested the local coffin-maker, a good judge of shape and size, but was shouted down.

The discussion was at this interesting stage when in walked three old Doon School boys, vintage early 1950s, all known to Nandu. They went to a table not far from where I was perched, and the conversation went something like this:

'Remember old Suri?'

'Hyderabad House, wasn't he?'

'No. Tata.'

'I must be confusing him with Hari.'

'Hari was in Kashmir House. We were in the same dorm.'

'Oh, I thought you were in Jaipur House with Gulab.'

'No, you're confusing me with Nimbu. Gulab was in Hyderabad. Weren't you in Kashmir?'

'No, Jaipur.'

Nandu strolled over to take part in this stimulating conversation. Everyone remembers Nandu. He was in Tata, of course. Or was it Jaipur? Anyway, they chatted amiably about old Housemasters—Holdsworth and Hughes, Hensman and Gurdial—and someone recalled old —— who had a beautiful daughter, the only girl in the school!

Of course it was drinks on the house for the old boys, and as a result I went one drink short as Nandu was running out of whisky and gin and wasn't about to serve his V.S.O.P. cognac. Heaven-Born had been eyeing the cognac bottle for some time. It was his favourite, indeed his only drink, except when times were bad. But the glint in his eye had been detected by the Man-from-Sail, who whisked the bottle away in the interests of justice and fair play.

Heaven-Sent had been a silent but appreciative spectator and now, always a man who struck while the iron was hot (even if his hand got singed in the process), announced his intention of publishing a book on the public schools of India.

'A sure-fire bestseller,' I said. 'Take just fifty schools, and you'll have tens of thousands of old boys and girls queuing up for copies!'

The old boys in our midst met this proposal with

a frosty silence. Were there really other public schools in the land, they wondered. Well, possibly the Mayo. Jack Gibson had gone there after leaving the Doon, hadn't he? But they weren't aware of any others.

Nandu looked across at me and asked: 'And where did you do your schooling, Ruskin?'

'Greyfriars,' I said without any hesitation.

They took it quietly. There was a familiar ring about Greyfriars. A place of strong traditions, no doubt. Tucked away in the heart of old England, it had of course been the spiritual and physical home of the immortal Billy Bunter, Fat Boy of the Remove, but I did not tell them that. Why spoil the good impression I had made!

# By the Fireside

Last winter, I was sitting with Nandu and the Man-from-Sail, sipping cherry brandy in front of a crackling wood fire at Nandu's private sitting room at the Savoy. It was an idyllic scene, straight out of Dickens. You could say that I was Pickwick, the Man-from-Sail was Sam Weller, and Nandu was Mr Micawber; each of us had something in common with these characters.

Nandu hadn't used the cottage fireplace for some years, but since it was Christmas and bitterly cold outside, he thought it would be a good time for the supreme indulgence—a blazing wood fire in an old-fashioned fireplace.

And blaze it did! I hadn't enjoyed a really roaring fire in years. And the brandy was good too. So good that it took us some time to realize that those lovely crackling sounds were emanating from the roof as well as from the fireplace. The Man-from-Sail, always good for an emergency, dashed outside and came back shouting, 'The chimney's on fire!'

And so it was. We ran outside to find flames leaping into the night sky. The chimney, unused and uncleaned for fifty years, was ablaze and sparks were flying in all directions. It was all hands on deck, or rather on the roof, and it was a sight to watch dear Nandu cavorting around with a bucket of water. I went inside to make sure the brandy hadn't caught fire, poured myself a stiff one, and returned to join the firefighters, consisting of the late-night kitchen staff, most of whom had been celebrating Christmas in their own way.

The fire was brought under control before it could do any major damage, but Nandu no longer uses his fireplace. Instead, we find him huddled before an ineffectual electric heater, quite forgetting that it was electrical short-circuits that caused most of the major fires in Mussoorie and Simla over the past few years.

\* \* \*

Building a fire is an art and only a few people are really good at it. For if the wood is damp, or the chimney dirty, or the sticks carelessly placed, you could have a room full of smoke and a very frustrating evening.

Above all, make sure your chimney is in good condition. Keep it clean (Nandu should have done that) and you will have nothing to fear.

Our love of a wood fire is partly inherited. Our ancestors, near or remote, had nothing but wood to warm them; and the sight and scent of a wood fire may well stir in us long-buried racial memories.

No other fire lends such a variety of colour to its flames, casts such dancing shadows, breathes such fragrant scents or dies into so clean an ash as a log fire. It leads the imagination back in time. A wood fire entices into the mountains and great forests, beautiful in all seasons.

And it is romantic, too. I can remember sitting by the fire with a lovely girl beside me—oh, long years ago—holding her hands, looking into her eyes, and murmuring sweet words of love . . . Until a cold draught up my trousers told me that the fire had gone out. And by the time I had rekindled it, there was a knock at the door. Christmas revellers poured in and romance had to wait for another fire-lit evening.

# V

## LEAVES FROM A JOURNAL

# Leaves from a Journal

*9th May, 1997*

New moon in a deep purple sky.

*10th May*

Sal trees near Rajpur. A lovely sight—varying shades of green; new leaf freshened by recent rain.

Jacaranda time.

Returning to Mussoorie around midnight, saw a leopard leap over the parapet wall, then her three cubs scurrying into the bushes. I thought I'd seen my last leopard some years ago, but in the hills this is obviously an animal that knows how to survive.

*11th May*

Small boy in a bookshop thrust an Enid Blyton book at me, and asked me to sign it. So I signed 'Enid Blyton'. He seemed satisfied. I wouldn't mind changing sex if I could have her sales.

Dinner at Brahm Dev's. Amiable, elderly Colonel took my empty glass, poured me a whisky and soda, and then absent-mindedly drank it himself.

It was that kind of day. First I'm mistaken for Enid Blyton, and then someone pinches my badly-needed drink.

*16th May*

The sun warm on our backs. The sort of summer's day that H.E. Bates described so well—summer being brief in both England and the western Himalaya.

Siddharth (soon to be four) and I (soon to be sixty-four), scrambled up the hillside collecting daisies. I was so careful not to fall that I grasped a nettle and got badly stung. This is called growing old disgracefully.

*19th May*

Began my birthday with a hangover, which grew worse as the day progressed, due partly to some rather noisy people dropping in just to 'meet the author'.

A PR man for some industrial group, whose reading (he boasted) was limited to *India Today*, proceeded to drop names—everyone from Khushwant Singh to Prime Minister Gujral, whom he referred to as 'Inder'. I knew what to expect, because Prem had seen them approach, and from my open window I'd heard the wife exclaim, 'He *can't* be living in *this* tumbledown building!' Nevertheless, they proceeded to drink my tea and consume my patties (I couldn't get at one) and then of course he had to ask the usual question, 'Why don't you use a computer?' And to forestall a pointless argument I said, 'Can't afford one,' which is quite true.

Just then my friend Bill walked in and I let him take some of the flak. The visitors hadn't read anything of mine, and hadn't heard of Bill, so I wasn't quite sure what they were doing in my flat—perhaps they'd mistaken it for a wayside café, in which case I should have presented them with a bill.

Bill told them about 'Dick', an eccentric Englishman (Scotsman?) who lived in a shack below the *dhobi-ghat* and made a living by begging in the bazaar. Apparently he had a brilliant mind (so Bill says) and was one of the early computer scientists before he went off his rocker. Can't say I'm surprised.

After they left, the Sharma family from Dehra arrived with rasgullas and improved my mood.

*23rd May*

No doubt it was a great moment when Stanley met Livingstone, but could it have been as momentous as when Laurel first met Hardy? I am sure the latter have given humankind more pleasure than the explorer-missionary and the journalist. We still love Stan and Olly forty years after they passed on. How beautifully they worked together, and what joy they gave to cinema audiences all over the world. Chaplin was clever (too clever sometimes?), Buster Keaton and Harry Langdon could be quite brilliant, and some of the early British comedians (Will Hay, Sidney Howard) deserved to be better known; but Stan and Olly were *lovable*, and that's what made them unique.

And that reminds me—I must get rid of that sofa in the sitting room, the one that tilts slightly to one side and overbalances when someone of a heavy build sits in it. Last month, Mrs Joy, the wife of an under secretary, went over sideways and ended up on the floor—the first time in her life anything like that had happened to her, she said. I made the mistake of saying, 'Well, there's a first time for everything,' and she left in a bit of a huff.

I try to warn people about the sofa, saying, 'Careful—that chair's a bit wobbly,' but when unexpected visitors come crashing in, I get a little confused and forgetful.

*25th May*

Elderly gentleman from Saharanpur, 'in search of conversation', got me off my bed (where I had been recovering from a two-day viral fever), and told me that he had always followed my career with interest and that his favourite story was my 'The Lamp Is Lit Again'.

I have never written a story with that title, but I forbore from saying so, not wishing to prolong the conversation. It is, in fact, a nice title, and I shall certainly use it some day!

He then told me that he was aware that my father had been in the ICS, something of which I was unaware. Poor Dad! He had been teacher, tea planter, English tutor and Air Force Officer (in that order), but he had never aspired to the Civil Service. I think what he wanted most was to have the world's best stamp collection, and I recall that he had a very fine collection of stamps. He had sold some before he died, and I don't know what happened to the rest.

My visitor having gone (with promises to return), I watered my plants—drooping after a spell of hot dry weather—and returned to my bed. Then Siddharth returned from school, jumped on my stomach, and demanded a story. I tried to oblige, but he complained that the story was too short. My publishers usually say the same thing.

*29th May*

The warm winds of summer are pleasant and relaxing but they also bring fevers and illness. An intermittent fever laid me low again, and I spent a few restless nights. Found some relief from sleeplessness by changing ends, placing my pillow at the foot of the bed and lying south to north instead of the usual north to south. Not only did I sleep better this way, I also had some vivid dreams. Insomniacs might try this method when all else fails.

*2nd June*

Dear HH ('Her Highness' of yore) is great fun over a few drinks, especially when she gets going on all the disasters that have overtaken her friends and acquaintances: P was knocked down by a truck; Y was sucked into the fuselage of an aeroplane; T has succumbed to an overdose of drugs and alcohol . . . She gives an excellent description of old S, a retired mountaineer, suffering from Alzheimer's and searching for Annapurna base camp on the Delhi Ridge. All with great sympathy and yet a certain relish. Anyone who is someone in Delhi now goes to a psychiatrist, she tells me, including one of her golfing friends, Mrs B, who is convinced that in her former life she was a golf ball.

As far as I can recall, Delhi did not have a single psychiatrist thirty years ago. No one was rich enough to afford such a luxury. Or perhaps no one was nutty enough. Now there are hundreds of psychiatrists, and thousands of affluent patients who imagine they were once Mughal emperors, famous courtesans, Ming vases, or golf balls.

### 6th June

Ennui . . . Tried hard, but couldn't shake it off. Then the smell of frying onions comes from the kitchen, where Beena is preparing lunch. This perks me up. There's nothing like frying onions to bring me to life again.

Often, the anticipation of a good meal is better than the meal itself.

### 8th June

A TV team arrived last evening while I was out, and left a message that they'd come over at ten this morning to interview me. Beena and Dolly tidied up the rooms, and at ten I was ready, shaved, and wearing a clean shirt. At 11 a.m. I received a phone call, saying could they come at 1 p.m., after lunch. I agreed; had my lunch, waited. At 3 p.m. a van rolled up with eight or nine camera crew and technicians, but no producer or interviewer. The lady hasn't arrived as yet,' they told me, meaning the producer. I blew my top and sent them all packing.

No sooner had they gone than I received a phone call from the producer to say she had just arrived. I told her about the fracas and she apologized. We agreed to do the interview tomorrow, at 10 a.m.

This is the last time I give a TV interview. Better to die in obscurity than become a raving lunatic in a celebrity-mad world.

*9th June*

The interview went off all right, except that after three hours of talking (to Sunit Tandon, a gentle soul) I felt quite exhausted. Siddharth came home from school and did his best to wreck their equipment. They left me with a cheque—quite a decent sum—the first time I've been paid for giving an interview. I almost said, 'Come again!' But let it be the last.

*14th June*

My forty-five-year-old Olympia typewriter is finally showing signs of ageing. Mrs Goel, who is Swiss, kindly lent me her old Travel Writer, a sturdy machine, but forgot to tell me it was a German-language typewriter. The letters y and z were interchanged (probably because z is used more frequently in German) with the result that I went quite mad, turning out sentences like this one:

'A zoung man sipped his brandz on the vozage to Yanyibar.'

Couldn't get the hang of it, so gave up. I suppose I ought to get a computer like everzone who is anzone (sorry, everyone who is anyone), but instead I bought myself two nice fountain pens with a resolve to improve my handwriting.

*15th June*

All of middle-class northern India appears to be trying to get into Mussoorie at once, to play video game, consume mountains of ice cream, and drop plastic bags into the Kempty waterfall. There are about 200 hotels and all of them filled to capacity. Those who live and work here have to put up with an influx of friends and relatives, who conveniently forget them when winter comes round. The traffic jams are horrendous. It's quicker to walk. But most people have forgotten how to walk. At this rate our legs will atrophy, and a few generations from now the human race will have to manage without legs or, at the very best, extremely short ones.

*11th June*

All telephones out of order for three days. Apparently a road cleaner, finding an exposed underground cable getting in the way of his work, decided that the best way to deal with the obstacle was to cut through it with a saw. This he did most effectively, demonstrating that the Stone Age has finally caught up with the Computer Age.

I have to admit to being something of a Stone Age man myself; never could manage or control anything on wheels. Falling off bicycles was a regular occurrence during my boyhood. And later, my attempt to learn to drive a Land Rover ended with my smashing through a single-brick boundary wall in New Delhi's posh Friends Colony, stopping only a few metres from where a sumptuous open-air lunch party was in progress. I wrote a story about it, in which they asked me to stay for lunch; but in reality, they made me pay for the wall.

\*\*\*

Beena buys a lot of second-hand cane furniture from a departing Woodstock teacher. It fills up the sitting room and to my dismay I find that she has thrown out the wobbly sofa that used to tip over and deposit its occupant on the floor—my last defence against the unwanted visitor!

*25th June*

Some genuine early-monsoon rain, warm and humid, and not that cold high altitude stuff we've been having all year. The plants seem to know it too, and the first cobra-lily rears its head from the ferns as I walk up to the bank and post office.

The mist affords a certain privacy

A schoolboy asked me to describe the hill station and valley in one sentence, and all I could say was: 'A paradise that might have been.'

\* \* \*

In the vicinity of the bank, one occasionally meets the odd retired executive, now 'consultant' in business management, still very prosperous, usually with adult children studying abroad, and yet, in spite of all he's got, exuding a strong aroma of failure. People like him long for a pat on the back, but there's no one to give it to them.

\* \* \*

Visited HH and got news of fresh disasters:

1. Large number of tourists down with food poisoning after dining at a new hotel.

2. Abnormal nephew talks to the wall and flaps his arms like a bird. (I feel like doing this myself, sometimes.)

3. Young Prem lala, who fell off a roof and damaged his spine and skull, may never recover. (Six months later: I'm glad to be able to say that he did.)

I had gone over looking for something to cheer me up, but even Bill looked gloomy and his purple socks failed to stimulate.

## 29th June

Publishers seldom enjoy sending out royalty statements, or the cheques that accompany them. The author Frank Swinnerton once gave this description of the publisher J.M. Dent, for whom he worked at one time: 'He was a very emotional man. One day I went into his office when he was signing royalty cheques, and the tears were running down his cheeks.'

Not every publisher is heartbroken when he signs a cheque, but I have noticed a certain stinginess among those who run one-man shows. It is a character trait which probably goes back to the anal-retentive stage when as children they derived pleasure and power from withholding their faeces.

I know at least one Delhi publisher who derives a sadistic pleasure from withholding his authors' royalties. And there was one desperate character who got himself admitted into the cardiac unit of a hospital whenever royalty time came around. 'The patient cannot be disturbed,' were the familiar words of the medic in charge. This went on for several years, until he had no writers left apart from me. He has promised to send me something on account of royalties provided I help him pay his hospital bills.

*1st July*

Reading to four-year-old Siddharth from *Alice in Wonderland*, or rather retelling the story with the help of the illustrations, I was surprised by the hold that it can have on an imaginative child. For several evenings he has been demanding *Alice*—he particularly likes the 'Drink Me' potion and its spectacular results, the Mad Hatter, the pool of tears, and of course the Cheshire cat. Has even taken to drinking his soup, provided I recite 'Beautiful Soup' while he is at it! I used to think *Alice* was for adults or sophisticated older children, but I can see now that small children would be fascinated by a world in which nothing can be taken for granted. Lively illustrations do help. I wonder how many artists since Tenniel have tried their hand at *Alice*—several hundred, I should think. My only criticism of Anthony Browne's illustrations is that he introduces his own characters (for instance, a gorilla) who are not in the book.

*16th July*

The last fortnight taken up with correcting proofs of my little memoir, and fleshing it out here and there; also proofs of one of my children's books. And then tax returns, obligatory at this time of the year. Switching from the story of a mountain leopard to doing an income tax return is rather daunting, and rather like one of Alice's adventures. Come to think of it, I'd rather face a leopard than an income tax inspector.

## Leaves from a Journal

### 21st July

Jolly evening at HH's in spite of the news that her grand-nephew was in a mental hospital, her business partner (in Bombay) was dying from lymph cancer, and almost every acquaintance was either expiring or in a bad way financially

She is of course immune to all the disasters that surround her. Is fond of me but would never give me any money because she says I would squander it. And of course she's right—I would!

Ganesh did her a service, so she has promised him a new car. That is, if Nandu (of the Savoy) pays half.

### 30th July

Book completed, tax return submitted. Celebrated by taking a hot bath and sleeping all day

My action justified by BBC Science report that our immune system works best when we are sleeping. That afternoon siesta's all important! (Mexican proverb: 'Oh to do nothing, and then to rest.')

### 12th August

Endless rain, and a permanent mist. We haven't seen the sun for eight or nine days. Everything damp and soggy. Nowhere to go. Pace the room, look out of the window at a few bobbing umbrellas. At least it isn't cold rain. The hillsides are lush as late-monsoon flowers begin to appear—wild balsam, dahlias, begonias and ground orchids.

The day's routine carries on. Rakesh goes off in the taxi and gets a fare once in three days. Dolly and

Siddharth go to school, come home wet. Prem takes his father to the Community hospital for a check-up. I sit at my desk, pen in hand, waiting for the elusive moment of inspiration, but all I get is a persistent mosquito hovering around my head. How did it get up here, to these cooling heights? In the taxi, possibly. Or trapped in the boot of a tourist's car. My last visitor, three days ago, drove up from hot and steamy Saharanpur, and might well have brought a few mosquitoes with him. This one seems to like my room. Should I swat it? Or be the good Jain monk and let it live a little longer? If it's a Saharanpur mosquito, it won't survive up here. So I open my window and encourage it to fly back to Saharanpur. But it doesn't care for the mist. It settles on the page of an open book. On an impulse, I snap the book shut. End of mosquito. I look at the title of the book. It's called *The Consolation of Philosophy*.

\* \* \*

Browsing through some of my old books (early Penguins, in fact) I came across this passage in Laura Knight's autobiography, *Oil Paint and Grease Paint* (1936):

'Something inside the artist drives him, a power transcends himself, and only in the soil of complete humility can an artist grow—I am blind, I would see; I am deaf, I would hear; I am a little child, I would know.

'Conceived in humility and awe, born in pain—thus Art comes forth.'

\* \* \*

A few years ago, I found myself under arrest. A story I had written had offended the guardians of our morals, and the result was a criminal charge. But this is not an account of how I was pursued by the law because of my sensual literary style. Unpleasant experiences are best forgotten if one is not to become a bitter old cynic. And, in any case, I was finally acquitted.

No one who is under arrest is likely to enjoy the experience. Warrants make bad reading, except in detective stories. So how does a writer of essays and light verse take it? A nervous breakdown would not have been surprising, and did in fact seem likely. But I was saved from one by the swallows.

Yes, the swallows.

There I was, sitting on a hard bench on the police station veranda, waiting for a couple of friends to arrive and stand bail for me, when I noticed the swallows wheeling in and out of the veranda, busily building a nest in the eaves of the old building. Nothing unusual about that. Swallows love old police stations. But just because it was so usual, so commonplace, I took heart.

The right word is *reassuring*. That is what we all need when we are in a tight corner—a little reassurance. Like a friendly, familiar face. Or the sleepy drone of a cricket commentary in the background. Or someone whistling cheerfully in a gloomy corridor. Something to let you know that even if things seem to be getting out of hand for a while, the rest of the world is still going on quite normally. And for me, nothing could have been more reassuring than the sight of several swallows—all oblivious to the terrors of the *thana*—going about their business.

178

Business as usual. That's what reassures. It bucked me up tremendously, just watching those little birds.

Presently an official came along, took me into his office, and asked me to fill in a form. I remarked, 'Have you noticed that the swallows are nesting in the veranda?' He looked at me blankly. He hadn't noticed any swallows. What *were* swallows, anyway? Obviously I was deranged—a candidate for an asylum and not for a jail.

But I knew then, watching the blank look on his face, that I was equal to the situation—that I was dealing with a human being whose plight was worse than mine, because he would never be able to find reassurance so quickly or so easily.

*20th August*

The little rose begonia. It has a glossy chocolate leaf, a pretty rose-pink flower, and it grows and flowers in my bedroom—almost all the year round. What more can one ask for?

Some plants become friends. Most garden flowers are fair-weather friends; gone in the winter when times are difficult up here in the mountains. Those who stand by you in adversity—plant or human—are your true friends; there aren't many around, so cherish them and take care of them in all seasons.

A loyal plant friend is the variegated ivy that has spread all over my bedroom wall. My small bedroom-cum-study gets plenty of light and sun, and when the windows are open, a cool breeze from the mountains floats in, rustling the leaves of the ivy. (This breeze can turn into a raging blizzard in winter— on one occasion, even blowing the roof away—but right now, it's just a zephyr, gentle and balmy.) Ivy plants seem to like my room, and this one, which I brought up from Dehra Dun, took an instant liking to my desk and walls, so that I now have difficulty keeping it from trailing over my typewriter when I am at work.

I like to take in other people's sick or discarded plants and nurse or cajole them back to health. This has given me a bit of a reputation as a plant doctor. Actually, all I do is give an ailing plant a quiet corner where it can rest and recuperate from whatever ails it—they have usually been ill-treated in some way. Plant abuse, no less! And it's wonderful how quickly a small tree or plant will recover if given a little encouragement.

I rescued a dying asparagus fern from the portals of the Savoy Hotel, and now, six months later, its strong feathery fronds have taken over most of one window, so that I have no need of curtains. Nandu, the owner of the Savoy, now wants his fern back.

Maya Banerjee's sick geranium, never allowed to settle in one place—hence its stunted appearance—has, within a fortnight of being admitted to my plant ward, burst forth in such an array of new leaf and flower that I'm afraid it might pull a muscle or strain a ligament from too much activity.

Should I return these and other plants when they have fully recovered? I don't think they want to go back. And I should hate to see them suffering relapses on being returned to their former abodes. So I tell the owners that their plants need monitoring for a while . . . Perhaps, if I sent in doctor's bills, the demands for their return would not be so strident?

Loyalty in plants, as in friends, must be respected and rewarded. If dandelions show a tendency to do well on the steps of the house, then that is where they shall be encouraged to grow. If sorrel is happier on the window sill than on the hillside, then I shall let it stay, even if it means the window won't close properly. And if the hydrangea does better in my neighbour's garden than mine, then my neighbour shall be given the hydrangea. Among flower lovers, there must be no double standards. Generosity, not greed; sugar, not spite.

And what of the rewards for me, apart from the soothing effect of fresh fronds and leaves at my place of work and rest? Well, the other evening I came home to find my room vibrating to the full-throated chorus of several crickets who had found the ivy to their liking. I thought they would keep me up all night with their music; but when I switched the light off, they immediately fell silent: So, crickets don't sing in the dark, I surmised, and switched the light on again. Once more, I was treated to symphonic variations on a theme by Tchaikovsky.

This reminded me that I hadn't listened to Tchaikovsky for some time, so I played a tape or The Dance of the Sugar Plum Fairy' from the *Nutcracker Suite*. The crickets maintained a respectful silence, even with the lights on.

Last night, a beetle flew in at the open window and landed with a plop in my jug of drinking water. He didn't appear to be a good swimmer, so I picked him up and flung him back into the night. One has to draw the line somewhere.

*21st August*

Sometimes I live with a deepening sense of failure.

After forty years of writing, very little money and not much recognition outside India. But I have sung my songs and told my tales, and I doubt if I would have done any better in other circumstances.

As a boy, reading was my religion. It helped me to discover my soul. Later, writing helped me to record its journey.

## 24th August

The sun comes out, and a yellow butterfly alights on the red dahlia.

From my window I see that the Song river with a goodly flow of water is heading for its junction with the Ganga. All the streams and rivulets are in spate. Soon it will be flood time in the plains.

Took Siddharth by the hand and walked home with him. Something I had often done with his father (Rakesh) just over twenty years ago. Now *that's* an achievement! Just a small one . . .

\* \* \*

At night, the lights of Dehra are spread all over the valley. Over the years, I've watched the town grow from a small cluster of lights to a city by night. It is at its prettiest from a distance. At close quarters, the odours from the rubbish dumps overpower the scent of the jasmine and *raat-ki-rani*. Mussoorie is not much better. Refuse, sewage and plastic all have to go somewhere—and that isn't very far.

*6th September*

Three days of incessant rain. A powdery film of mildew covers the frayed old carpet in the Savoy Bar; it is now as green as the billiard table. A fusty, musty odour pervades the airless room. Ganesh and I do our best to imbue it with some life. There have been no visitors for days, unless you count the little shrew that meanders between the chairs and tables. People say the shrew *(chhuchhunder)* is lucky, or rather, brings luck. Maybe I'll take it home one of these days. Nandu says to leave it—his need is greater than mine.

To relieve the tedium, we visit HH who has already informed me (on the phone) that she is severely depressed by Princess Diana's funeral which she has been following on TV. We find her cheerful enough, and she enlarges on her favourite theme of violent death, giving us tales of murder, suicide and misadventure in various princely families she has known. Poisonings were popular, followed by 'hunting' accidents.

Today, violent crime has shifted to political, business and entertainment circles. And poisonings and accidental deaths are passé. You simply contact a gang of hired killers (or kidnappers) who do the job for you. Rates are negotiable. And of course you might end up as one of their victims one day.

We shall miss HH when she leaves next week.

Speaking of an old flame, she remarks, 'It was Y — who taught me to drink.'

'And you were a quick learner,' adds Bill.

For which remark he will have to hide in the shrubbery for a day.

*15th September*

Glorious hot sunshine greets us this morning, and I resolve to do nothing but bask in it.

Twelve noon: Resolve has been undertaken.

One p.m. Clouds move in.

Thought HH had gone, but received a merry call from her to say goodbye once again and to continue, 'Let me tell you about the latest tragedies that have taken place.'

First, Bill's mother had died, as well as one of his aunts, but as they were both over ninety, Bill wasn't too upset.

Second, her caretaker's TB treatment in Delhi had cost over ten thousand rupees and he still had the disease!

In spite of the recent horrendous train accident, HH is travelling by train to Delhi. Look forward to seeing her next year.

*21st September*

Nandu and old Negi running the Savoy almost by themselves, as most of the staff have rendered themselves *hors de combat* due to various alcohol-related incidents.

Ram Singh, the driver, had an all-night booze session with the night chowkidar, as a result of which the chowkidar has a black eye and Ram Singh has injuries to his ribcage. Then the gardener went for the *masalchi* who, being younger, knocked the old man down. The gardener got stitches in his forehead and lodged a report with the police, as a result of which the *masalchi* decided it was time to visit his ailing father in Bijnor.

Not that the hotel is exceptional. I have an alcoholic postman. And after ten p.m. almost half the town is drunk. Let's put it down to global warming.

*3rd October*

We have gone straight from monsoon into winter rain. Snow at higher altitudes.

After an evening hailstorm, the sky and hills are suffused with a beautiful golden light.

*18th October*

Monkey population has increased, probably faster than the human population, at least on this hillside. Got up in the morning, opened the door to the bathroom, and found one sitting on the loo. It wasn't using the loo, just relaxing upon it. I shut the door hurriedly, then banged on it several times until the monkey left via the window.

And a week ago I found one at the telephone, rifling through my phone book. It made off with the book and sat on the parapet wall, trying to chew it. When it found the book inedible, it flung it away. The *sabziwala* rescued the book, somewhat battered but still intact.

I notice the phone bill has gone up this month. Maybe that monkey actually got through, long-distance, to some distant relative in the plains.

\* \* \*

185

The spiders on my bedroom wall gave rise to the
following lines:

> This little spider,
> His name is Paul;
> He loves to crawl all over my wall.
>
> This little spider,
> His name is Bhim;
> His legs are quite long,
> But he doesn't swim.
>
> Here's a third spider,
> Her name is Sue;
> And if she gets hungry,
> She'll eat those two!

*\* \* \**

In a month of fluctuating moods, some of the things
I have enjoyed:

Three bright orange nasturtiums taking the sun at
my window.
Tuning in at random to a BBC request programme
and hearing Nelson Eddy sing 'Rose Marie'.
Watching Shrishti grow quite pretty.
Getting a cheque in the mail.

*15th November*

*Scenes from a Writer's Life* was published and slipped
quietly into a few bookshops, minus fanfare or any
kind of pre-publicity. A copy went to my first

publisher, Diana Athill, and I received the following response:

'My dear Ruskin,

I can't imagine a better Christmas-cum-eightieth-birthday present than the arrival of the copy of *Scenes from a Writer's Life* which you so kindly asked Penguin to send me. I was just about to leave London for the cottage in Norfolk which once belonged to an aunt of mine and which now her daughter and I share as a country retreat, when the parcel arrived; and the first thing I did when I got here was read it in one greedy gulp. I enjoyed—and of course still enjoy—it so much. That 'simple and immensely moving' style has remained untarnished, just with a nice little edge added to it at the appropriate moments—e.g. your account of Ms Manning and her fire-extinguishing lover, which made me laugh out loud. It was very interesting to be told about your childhood, rather an extraordinary sensation to come face to face with my past self, and enormously gratifying to be reminded that the dark horse (more like a little dark *pony* in those days!) on whom we placed our only-too-modest bet went on to establish himself so securely as a writer.

I had conveniently forgotten, and blushed hotly at being reminded, how *dreadfully* we kept you hanging about. It was Andre's worst habit—liking something well enough to want it on his list, then dragging his feet with it because of doubting its commercial viability. And I now think it was shockingly feeble of me not to fight him more fiercely whenever this happened (you were far from being the only victim). But at the time I suppose I lacked confidence in some way, because as I remember it I just felt helpless. Unhappy but helpless. May I now say *Sorry!* for that long-ago anxiety and frustration we caused you, and hope that subsequent success has made the scar fade . . .'

### 23rd November

Dinner party at an official's residence in Dehra. Women were uniformly attractive; men looked as though they had seen better days. Best-looking male was the hired waiter.

### 25th November

I must be a very dull sort of fellow because whenever anyone meets me on the road past my home, they invariably ask after Victor or Tom or Steve or Sunny or any of the other celebrities who live up here or pop in and out of the hill station from time to time.

Only last week a boy and a girl came up to me and asked, 'Are you Victor Banerji?'

'You must have seen my earlier films,' I snarled, and hurried on before they could discover their mistake.

And a day or two afterwards, a pretty girl wearing what looked like football stockings sidled up to me and asked, 'Doesn't Tom Alter live somewhere here?'

'Only when he's out of work,' I said.

Both Victor and Tom are delightful persons and I am more than happy to point out the way to their homes, knowing full well that they hate casual callers.

One day Tom and I were talking about *Junoon*, a

film based on my novella called *A Flight of Pigeons.*
Tom had a small role in the film—about two or three
minutes of acting—and he told me he received ten
thousand rupees for doing the scene. This is exactly
what I received for the entire story—a good example
of the value Bollywood places on writers.

*Junoon* wasn't a bad film, but some of my
experiences in the film world are memorable for all
the wrong reasons. There was the producer who
bought one of my wildlife stories and actually made
the film; Tom Alter was in it again, this time as a
wicked foreign shikari out to decimate the tiger
population.

Unfortunately, halfway through the film his fellow
shikari actually got mauled by a tiger and the story
had to be changed to fit the circumstances. This was
all right, but then the circus tiger which was playing
the main role of a tiger in the wild caught pneumonia
and died and the film was completed with a substitute
tiger which was a bad actor. The film was never
released.

About ten years ago the Children's Film Society
of India bought one of my stories. It is still under
production. And I am told there is a shortage of good
stories for children's films.

But the most memorable experience was the
children's film made here by an Australian director of
dubious credentials. I can't complain about the fee
because the film, when completed, bore little or no
resemblance to the story. Nor did the actors even
resemble themselves.

The producer hadn't done his homework, because
he had neglected to ascertain that the leading lady
was in fact three or four months pregnant. Now the

action of the entire story (a simple one when I wrote it) all took place in the course of a single day, but of course they took three months to make the film and all the while the leading lady grew more and more rotund, rather like Alice in Wonderland on the wrong pills.

When the completed film was previewed, she was seen to change shape in a rapid succession of takes—shapely as Garbo in one scene, round as a barrel in the next. This, too, was never released.

* * *

If mice could roar
And elephants soar
And trees grow up in the sky;
If tigers could dine
On biscuits and wine,
And the fattest of men could fly!
If pebbles could sing
and bells never ring
And teachers were lost in the post;
If a tortoise could run
And losses be won,
And bullies be buttered on toast;
If a song brought a shower,
And a gun grew a flower,
This world would be nicer than most!

# ENVOI

## THE LAMP IS LIT

# When the Lamp Is Lit

*'Love thy art, poor as it may be, which thou hast learned,
and be content with it; and pass through the rest of life
like one who has entrusted to the gods with his whole soul
and all that he has, making thyself neither the tyrant nor
the slave of any man.'*

Marcus Aurelius (AD 121-180), the last of the great
Antonine emperors, speaks to us across the centuries
through his *Meditations*, those nuggets of wisdom
jotted down during a crowded and adventurous life.

Being unable to find much comfort or wisdom in
the utterances of present-day teachers, preachers, or
godmen (be they of the Eastern or Western variety), I
frequently turn for advice and reassurance to the early
Greek and Roman philosophers—Epicurus, Epictetus,
Marcus Aurelius, Seneca and others—those Stoics and
Epicureans whose precepts are as relevant today as
they were during the finest flowering of the Greek
and Roman civilizations.

'Love thy art, poor as it may be . . .' I have never
regretted following this precept; for, no matter how
skilful one is with words, it is only drudgery to have
to use them in the more mundane spheres of
journalism. I have tried to use words creatively and
lovingly. The gift for putting together words and
sentences to make stories or poems or essays has
carried me through life with a certain serenity and
inner harmony which could not have come from any
unloved vocation.

Within my own 'art' I think I have known my

limitations and worked within them, thus sparing myself the bitter disappointment that comes to those whose ambitions stretch far beyond their talents. Do what you know best, and do it well. Act impeccably. Everything will then fall into place.

I was looking for a living example to try and illustrate this precept, and came across it in the persons of Mahboob Khan and Ramji Mal, stonemasons who were engaged in restoring Shah Jahan's Hall of Mirrors in the Agra Fort. They had been at work for ten years, slowly but deftly bringing their epic task to completion.

The restoration work was so intricate that these two skilled craftsmen could restore only about six inches in a day. In recreating the original stucco-work on walls and ceiling, everything had to be done impeccably: millions of pieces of tiny mirrors and coloured glass had to find their exact place in order to reflect just the right amount of light and, at the same time, conform to a certain pattern.

It is a small art, theirs, but it requires infinite patience, skill and dedication. No fame for them, no great material reward. Their greatest reward comes from the very act of taking pains in the pursuit of perfection.

Surely they must be happy, or at least contented men. In truth, I am yet to meet a neurotic carpenter or stonemason or clay-worker or bangle-maker or master craftsman of any kind. Those who work with wood or stone or glass are usually well-balanced people. Working with the hands is in itself a therapy. Those of us who work with our minds—composers or artists or writers—must try to emulate these craftsmen's methods, paying attention to every detail and working with loving care.

The trouble is that creative people are cerebral creatures with fluctuations of mood that make life exhilarating at one moment and depressing the next. And this is often reflected in their work unless they have become mechanical, turning out books or paintings like samosas.

Yet there are times when I do love my art. And because I have loved it, I think I have been able to pass through life without being any man's slave or tyrant. I doubt if I have ever written a story or essay or workaday article unless I have really wanted to write it. And in this way I have probably suffered materially, because I have never attempted a blockbuster of a novel, or a biography of a celebrity, or a soap opera that goes on for ever. The prospect of spinning out thousands of words of little or no consequence seems a dull and dreary way of earning a living.

'Writing is easy,' said Red Smith. 'All you have to do is sit at your typewriter till little drops of blood appear on your forehead.' That's true for some of us. But I refuse to suffer. At the first sign of drops of blood or perspiration, I get up from my desk and do something totally different—make myself a sandwich, water my ferns, take a walk, or discuss politics with the milkman. If the writing isn't easy, if I'm not enjoying it, I know I'm better off doing something else.

And yet writing is easy if I'm happy with my theme. Ask me to write a piece on petunias, and I'll turn out an enthusiastic essay on this underrated flower. I might even write a story about someone who grows petunias, because such a person must obviously have sterling qualities. I might even delve into the love life of a petunia-grower because those who love flowers must, by their very nature, be loving, even sensual and passionate people. From *The Rose Garden* of Sa'adi to Wordsworth's sea of golden daffodils, love poetry and song has been enriched by flowers—the rose, the jasmine, the lily, the daffodil, the honeysuckle . . . No sweeter scent than the honeysuckle's. No more inviting name. Come, suckle up to your honey, it seems to say; and under my bower you'll kiss the fleeting hours away.

Of flowers, lovers, melons and moonbeams, I can write reams. But ask me to write the life story of a great leader or media tycoon or matchbox-maker, and I'm stumped and stymied. Those little drops of blood threaten to appear. I cannot breathe life into these subjects, noble though they might be. Their true personalities, the essence of their natures, somehow eludes me. It is not that they are too complicated, but rather that one has to peel off too many layers of protective armour to get at the flesh and blood that lies beneath the skin. In the case of the great leader, all those speeches—no matter how many fat volumes they may occupy—are just so many layers of onion peel. And the more you peel the less you find. We come no nearer to the heart and mind of our hero.

As for the captains of industry, we have even less to go on. Factory chimneys, figures, television satellites, song charts, all go into your computers and come out neatly sanitized yet somehow faceless. What they felt like in their darker moments remains well hidden from posterity. It took the genius of

Shakespeare to reach into the darker recesses of the human mind, and he got no help from his subjects either; they were long dead when he wrote of their personal tragedies—for tragedy is usually the lot of those whose grasp exceeds their reach. Alexander, Caesar, Napoleon and other conquerors, when they forget that they are mortals must reckon with the gods: the gods being the self-destructive elements in their own natures.

Why is humility so hard to come by? Most religions teach the wisdom of humility, but who listens? We all know that life is finite, that human civilization, for what it's worth, is self-limiting. And yet the most educated of men will strut about their little world like actors on a stage; they assume the mantle of immortals, deluding themselves into thinking they are indispensable, until eventually they join all those other indispensables who have reached perfection in the form of dust or ashes.

Why so much pride when a little humility can get us far more by way of love and peace and happiness? Better to efface yourself like the cricket who is heard but seldom seen than to flap your wings and crow like a cockbird before ending up as someone's tandoori dinner.

Happiness is an elusive state of mind, not to be gained by clumsy pursuit. It is given to those who do not sue for it: to be unconcerned about a desired good is probably the only way to possess it.

'I enjoy life,' said Seneca, 'because I am ready to leave it.'

If we can disencumber ourselves of nine-tenths of our worldly goods, it should not be difficult to leave the rest behind. But it's amazing how most of us hang on to our bric-a-brac, hoping maybe that it will be treasured and valued by those who come after us. Yes, the Duke and Duchess of Windsor's slice of wedding cake, preserved for over fifty years, recently fetched over thirty thousand dollars at an auction in New York. But did the original royal owners have that end in mind when they decided to hang on to a slice of the cake that symbolized their bittersweet romance? It certainly wasn't put away as an investment. As a symbol of the sacrifice that Edward made in giving up the throne of England in exchange for Mrs Simpson, it certainly meant something to the ex-king and his wife; but to its subsequent and present owners it is merely a curiosity which has cost them a lot of money. Perhaps they will put it on display There are always people who will gaze in awe and wonder at such a thing. But I would like to see one of them eat it.

'How weary, stale, flat and unprofitable!' sighed Hamlet in another context, although he might well have been commenting on the values of our own time, which sets more store on a pop singer's toothbrush or a dead princess's wardrobe than on the legacy of the truly great. It's a world in which we elevate the second rate above the first rate. Will posterity set the record straight? Seedy politicians, swelling with self-importance, and the men who pull their strings, the medieval robber barons of today, will do their best to promote the second best, because that's where the money lies, but Time has a way of taking the stuffing out of the bully, the braggart and of course the stuffed shirt.

Recently a publishing giant and media tycoon

refused to publish a book because he was afraid it would offend his customers in China. In doing so, he had curtailed his own freedom, made himself the victim of his own overriding ambitions. As his empire grows, his personal freedom shrinks. There is too much to lose. He is stuck on the point of his own glittering star, as he channels the second rate into the homes of helpless millions.

Not long ago there was another media moghul (name forgotten now, as such names must be) who found his success so stale, flat and in the end unprofitable, that he threw himself off the stern of his expensive yacht, seeking oblivion in the ocean. His body was never found. A great many decent people lost their savings because of him, otherwise the world was no worse for his exit.

Let us, for a change, turn to someone of real worth, whose name is imperishable. She made no money and did not live long enough to enjoy her fame. Riddled with tuberculosis she clung on to life until she finished her single masterpiece, *Wuthering Heights*, thereby giving to the world her very lifeblood along with the creative urge that justified her existence. Emily Brönte's indifference to wealth, fame, and personal comfort would be rare in today's world of high-powered literary agents and media hype. For her, writing was ecstasy. It was emancipation wrought in the soul. She and her sisters and others like them held only a brief tenure on this earth—no time to think of getting to the top of the ladder!—but their words, their thoughts, their songs are still with us. At least with those of us who would listen . . .

And there are many brave and good Indian

writers, who work in their own language—be it
Bengali or Oriya or Telugu or Marathi or fifteen to
twenty others—and plough their lonely furrow
without benefit of agent or media blitz or Booker prize.
Some of them may despair. But even so, they work
on in despair. Their rewards may be small, their
readers few, but it is enough to keep them from
turning off the light. For they know that the pen, in
honest and gifted hands, is mightier than the grave.

\* \* \*

And these are my parting words to you, dear Reader:
May you have the wisdom to be simple, and the
humour to be happy.

# Raindrop

This leaf, so complete in itself,
Is only part of the tree.
And this tree, so complete in itself,
Is only part of the forest.
And the forest runs down from the hill to the sea,
And the sea, so complete in itself,
Rests like a raindrop
In the hand of God.

# Acknowledgements

My thanks to:
Ravi Singh, of Penguin India, for his editorial help; the editors of *The Statesman* (New Delhi and Calcutta), *Deccan Herald* (Bangalore), *Hindu* (Chennai), *The Hindustan Times* (New Delhi), *Economic Times* (Calcutta), *Gentleman* (Mumbai), *Femina* (Mumbai), and the *Chirstian Science Monitor* (Boston), for first publishing some of this material.